Tales from the Dallas Mavericks

Jaime Aron

Sports Publishing L.L.C.
www.SportsPublishingLLC.com

Director of production: Susan M. Moyer
Developmental editor: Doug Hoepker
Project manager: Greg Hickman
Copy editors: Cynthia L. McNew and Holly Birch
Dust jacket design: Kerri Baker

ISBN: 1-58261-563-2

Printed in the United States.

SPORTS PUBLISHING L.L.C.
www.SportsPublishingLLC.com

To my Big Three:

Zachary, the original superstar,
and miracle men Jake and Josh.

Acknowledgments

Recalling 23 seasons of Dallas Mavericks basketball wouldn't have been possible without the help of many people.

The caretakers of the team's archives were a tremendous asset, both for the work they did then and their personal involvement now. Original public relations director Kevin Sullivan and his successor Tony Fay both took this project to heart and went out of their way to keep me pointed in the right directions. Their input was invaluable, as was walking Mavs encyclopedia Keith Grant. And if this was a box score instead of a book, there also would be lots of assists next to the names Dawn Holgate, Sarah Melton and Gregg Elkin of the current staff.

I'd also like to thank Mark Cuban for writing the foreword and everyone who shared their insight and memories. Kudos also to Danny Bollinger and Tony Gutierrez for going out of their way to help with pictures.

Special mention also goes to the folks at Sports Publishing L.L.C. for allowing me to delay this project by a year following the far-earlier-than-expected birth of my twin sons, Jake and Josh, whose amazing battle for their lives is the greatest comeback victory I've ever seen.

The final credits go to my oldest son, Zachary, for tolerating Daddy working on his book better than most five-year-olds would, and to my wife, Lori, whose support and dedication make it possible for me to pursue my dreams.

Contents

SECTION I:
The Original Glory Days (1978 to June 4, 1988)

SECTION II:
The Gory Days (June 5, 1988 to December 4, 1997)

SECTION III:
The New Glory Days (February 7, 1997 to Present)

Foreword

My collection of Mavericks memories began long before I bought the team. It started soon after I arrived in Dallas in the 1980s.

Having grown up in Pittsburgh, I had no local team to root for, so I became more a fan of the league. One of the perks of moving here was getting to go to NBA games.

I went to a lot of games during those years, which is how my love of the team really grew. It wasn't about wins and losses; I enjoyed the simple fun of being there. I appreciated the beauty of the game and the thrill of watching the best players in the world play my favorite game.

Of course, there are certain nights that stand out more than others.

The one I wish I could tell you all about was Moody Madness. But I wasn't there. I couldn't get a ticket.

I was there, though, when Roy Tarpley blew out his knee. I still remember wincing and feeling sick to my stomach.

Then came the miserable years. About the only good thing that came out of them was how easy it became to find a good seat, no matter what team the Mavs were playing.

I remember the Celtics coming to Reunion—I think it was during that awful 11-win season—and I got a floor seat for $10. The place was so empty that when Robert Parish went to the foul line, he could hear me heckling him about his weight. I suggested that "Chief" change his nickname to "Chubby," or something like that. He laughed so hard that he had to give the ball back to the ref before he shot.

Years later, I gave Charles Barkley an earful about how big he was getting. Every time he came down the floor, he spotted me and muttered some choice words.

I remember watching Popeye Jones going for 20 points and 20 rebounds in the same game and chanting "MVP! MVP!" Then there was the hope the Three Js brought, especially Jason Kidd. You've heard people say he makes players around him better. Well, he also made us fans better, because even when he was a rookie, just seeing the ball in his hands gave me the feeling that we were never out of a game.

Since moving from the front row to the front office, my perspective has changed. My enthusiasm hasn't. The difference is that now the overweight centers and aging power forwards know my name—and the commissioner pays attention when I heckle players (or refs).

Speaking of David Stern, he unintentionally provided me with some great memories.

Early into my ownership, he sat with me at a preseason game and said that I needed to tone down my enthusiasm. He said I should be careful because I was building up everyone's expectations—a bad idea, he said, because pro basketball is not an easy business. I remember looking at him and not saying anything, all the while thinking, "If that isn't motivation, I don't know what is!"

A few weeks later, I got to enjoy one of my first major thrills of ownership.

It happened in a November 2001 game against the Spurs at Reunion, two nights after Vancouver blew us out. Michael Finley hit a long jumper at the buzzer to win it 79-77, and we all burst onto the court to celebrate. Being an owner meant I could do that and not have to look over my shoulder for cops chasing me! I realized then how much more excitement I could have as an owner.

A second big thrill came later that season, when we played Utah in the playoffs.

Everyone remembers Calvin Booth's great shot that won Game 5. Well, it was an extra-sweet victory for me because of what happened earlier in the series.

In Game 2, John Stockton went to the foul line with 2.9 seconds left. After his second shot, the clock showed 2.2 left. I got very upset at the scorer, and when Jazz coach Jerry Sloan stood up, I blew him a kiss to let him know I wasn't angry with him. The commissioner later said that we probably lost that game because I was a distraction to the team. Then we won the next three games and the series.

As you can tell, I have a keen appreciation for the team's history because I lived through much of it, first as a Reunion Rowdy and now as an insider. But I'll always consider myself a fan—a Mavs Fan for Life.

Are you an MFFL? Here are some of the warning signs:

• Do you lose sleep after a loss?

• Are you so excited after we win that you can't tell enough people?

• If we've lost five in a row, are you 100 percent certain we're going to win the next game and just as sure there will be millions around the world jumping as well, all cheering on the Mavs?

If you're like me, you answered yes to all three. And if that's the case, you're going to love *Tales from the Dallas Mavericks*.

—Mark Cuban

Introduction

Want to know the best thing about the Dallas Mavericks?

No matter whether they've been great, awful or somewhere in between, they've always provided a stream of colorful personalities and quirky moments.

From a coach who brought a tiger into the locker room to contract negotiations held in a plane flying over Niagara Falls to a billionaire owner mixing up milkshakes, Mavericks history is far more interesting than you might expect out of a franchise whose greatest on-court achievement is coming within one game of reaching the NBA Finals.

The goal of this first-ever comprehensive team history was to blend the spirit of the Reunion Rowdies with the excitement of the team's three eras: the current glory days of Dirk Nowitzki, Michael Finley and Steve Nash; the original glory days of Mark Aguirre, Rolando Blackman and Derek Harper; and that in-between period best described as the gory days.

For this book of tales, it ended up being harder to decide what to leave out than what to include. All are part of what made this franchise what it is today.

The great thing about the tales format is that you can absorb it in either one long sitting or a bunch of short ones. Feel free to flip through for the events you remember—or maybe just the ones you don't.

Among the highlights:

• The full story of the serpentine path Donald Carter and Norm Sonju followed just to obtain an NBA team, including near-misses on relocating the Milwaukee Bucks, Buffalo Braves, and Kansas City Kings to Dallas.

• Memorable playoff wins such as the very first one, Moody Madness, the Game 5 victory over Utah to cap a coming-of-age comeback in 2001 and the two Game 7s in 2003.

• Regular-season classics including win number one, the first victory over Boston, Jason Kidd's performance in a double-overtime game against Houston that many believe helped him win Rookie of the Year, and the Unforgetta-Bull overtime win over two-time defending world champion Chicago in 1998.

• Disappointments such as Derek Harper dribbling out the clock in a playoff game against the Lakers, "The Wreck at the Hec" playoff series against Seattle in 1987, and the zero-field goal, two-point quarter in 1996.

• A fine-by-fine look at Mark Cuban's battles with the NBA, plus his day behind the counter at Dairy Queen and his night refereeing a Harlem Globetrotters game.

• All the times Don Nelson's name came up long before he was ever hired as GM.

• A breakdown of the first-round picks Dallas swindled from Cleveland in 1980 and how the Mavericks could've used those picks and their own to put together a roster featuring Karl Malone, Charles Barkley, Clyde Drexler *and* John Stockton.

• Other draft-related items, from the Jason Kidd vs. Grant Hill debate to the team's long, luckless history with the lottery.

• How the Three Js came together and fell apart, including the requisite Toni Braxton story and other details of just how bad the Mav-wrecks were in the 1990s.

• The first-ever published account of how the NBA's three-point contest started in Dallas.

• The rise of Brad Davis from journeyman to beloved icon and the sad sagas of Roy Tarpley and Leon Smith.

This franchise has gone through two arenas, three owners and seven head coaches. It's a team that was so good so fast that an NBA executive called it a "model" franchise. Then things got so bad that they were spoofed in a nationally syndicated cartoon.

Now the team is soaring again. Riding on their momentum is this book, *Tales from the Dallas Mavericks.*

Enjoy.

—Jaime Aron
August 2003

SECTION I:

The Original Glory Days

(1978 TO JUNE 4, 1988)

1

Birth of a Franchise

THE HUNT IS ON

Donald Carter had never been to an NBA game when he started pursuing a franchise. So he wasn't doing it to satisfy his love of basketball. And even though he was a multimillionaire businessman, he wasn't trying to pad his fortune or raise his profile. For Carter, it was simply a gift—to his hoops-loving wife, Linda, and to the city of Dallas, which he thought deserved to be considered "big-league" in every way.

The hunt began in 1978 when a group of California businessmen asked Carter—a multimillionaire thanks to Home Interiors & Gifts, the corporation his mother began two decades earlier—to be a minority partner in their bid to bring the NBA to Dallas.

The plan was to buy the Milwaukee Bucks and move them south. Although the existing owners demanded that Carter's group not talk about relocation until after the sale was approved, they were allowed to check with the league to make sure they'd be allowed to move the team. The response: No way.

"But they'd gotten my juices going," Carter said.

So Carter established a basketball office in Dallas, and in January 1979, he sent the league a $100,000 check for the local expansion rights. The group's goal was still to relocate an established team. But they got into the expansion process because "we didn't want someone to end-run us," Carter said.

Carter already had a point man in place, but wasn't convinced he had the right person. Then the Rev. W.A. Criswell recommended Norm Sonju. A year before, Sonju was president and general manager of the Buffalo Braves and tried moving them to Dallas. The team ended up in San Diego, and he ended up out of work.

Carter hired Sonju as GM in February 1979. His first assignment: Get a team.

That summer, a storm ripped the roof off Kemper Arena, home of the Kansas City Kings. That gave the Kings a chance to break their lease.

"Quick! Let's get them on the phone," Carter said.

Getting the Kings would've been a coup. Kansas City had just won the Midwest Division, Cotton Fitzsimmons had been named Coach of the Year, and guard Phil Ford had been Rookie of the Year.

"We flew them down the next day and made a deal. We had the club bought," Carter said. "Then we [went] back to the NBA and they again said no."

It was all about money. When a team moves, the rest of the league gets nothing. But when the league expands, the franchise fee is split among the owners.

Resigned to taking that route, the Dallas group offered in June 1979 to pay $8 million in cash. It was $1.5 million more than they would've paid for the Kings and $1.85 million more than the last expansion team paid. The league wanted $12 million and promised the first pick in the draft.

As negotiations dragged on, Carter was ready to give up. But then the group came up with an ownership formula based on 24 "units." Sonju and attorney Doug Adkins would automatically get one each, and they'd sell the other 22. Carter agreed to buy the first one. The league liked the plan enough that Sonju was told if he got the money, he'd get the team.

Having enough money behind the team was important, because in 1979 pro basketball was struggling. Most teams were in the red. There was no ESPN beaming highlights into homes every night, turning players into celebrities and cultural icons. In fact, the finals that season—and the next—were shown on tape delay, often after the results were given on the nightly news.

Sonju soon discovered that the richest people in Dallas weren't hoops junkies. He met with about 150 businessmen who had made their money all sorts of ways, and their three favorite sports were usually football, football and football. But Sonju was determined. He poured most of his time, and more than $250,000 of his own money, into trying to sell the remaining units. He even hired an employee: Rick Sund, a young scout/administrative assistant for the Milwaukee Bucks. Sund was named director of player personnel.

Then things got dicey. In January 1980, the expansion committee decided that if Dallas received a team, it would get the 11th pick of the draft, not the first. Then came word that some owners were skittish about expanding at all.

At a February meeting, commissioner Larry O'Brien took an informal vote. It revealed that seven teams were against Dallas's bid for a franchise. That was more than enough to squash Dallas's hopes. So O'Brien asked what it would take to make it work.

The other owners wanted to gain more money and to lose less talent; in the roster-stocking dispersal draft, they wanted to protect eight players instead of seven.

The shifting rules prompted many of Sonju's moneymen to back out. When he headed to a breakfast meeting with Carter and Adkins at a Coco's restaurant on the southwest corner of Midway and LBJ Freeway on April 15, 1980, the whole deal was shaky.

Carter, though, had come too far to let it fall apart.

"At this point, my wife and everyone were all excited," he said.

The founding fathers: Donald Carter (in white) signs the franchise charter agreement on May 1, 1980, alongside Norm Sonju (far left) and Doug Adkins (far right). NBA commissioner Larry O'Brien is between Carter and Adkins. (NBAE/Getty Images)

Carter admired Sonju's hard work and passion so much that he offered to buy the unsold units.

"It was pure emotion, not a business decision," Carter said soon after that milestone meeting.

Sonju wrote out the plans on a napkin and sent a formal proposal to the head of the expansion committee on Friday, April 25. They were willing to pay $2 million up front, $4 million in January, then $1.2 million for five years at 7 percent interest on the balance.

Sonju returned from lunch on Monday to find a message from a Phoenix Suns executive that read, "Congratulations. No need to return the call." The vote was 20-2 in favor of making Dallas the NBA's 23rd team. It was the first addition since 1974, and there wouldn't be another until 1988.

That same day—April 28,1980—Reunion Arena opened with the start of a weeklong World Championship Tennis event starring Jimmy Connors and John McEnroe.

An official announcement came May 1. The franchise agreement was signed, and the team name, colors and logo were unveiled that day.

"This is the end of a long and torturous route," O'Brien said, "and as I look here at Norm Sonju and [mayor] Bob Folsom, my God, it has been torturous."

The vision had become a reality. Now it was time to get to work. The dispersal draft was held May 28, giving Dallas 22 players. The Mavericks made their first trade and signed their first free agent June 9. The first regular draft was the next day, yielding 10 more players.

Five weeks later, Dick Motta became the first coach and Bob Weiss his assistant. Motta—a former NBA Coach of the Year who two summers before was celebrating a championship with Washington—provided instant credibility. His reputation for building winners helped buy time from local fans and gave outsiders reason to believe pro hoops might eventually catch on in football-frenzied Dallas. At the time the Cowboys were riding high as "America's Team," and the lowly Texas Rangers were the area's only other pro sports team.

Motta showed he was ready for the challenge with an enthusiastic introduction on July 17, 1980.

"When I heard of the expansion plans, my heart jumped 100 beats," he said. "This is the only time in my career I've actively campaigned for a job.

"We'll be a hustling, bustling team. I hope you'll be proud."

MR. C

It was only fitting that the Dallas Mavericks' first logo prominently featured a white cowboy hat hanging off the top right corner of a slanted M. Consider it a tip of the hat to franchise patriarch Don Carter—or "Mr. C," as he's belovedly known.

Standing tall at the top of the team's original hierarchy, Carter was a humble good old boy, as honest and reliable as his Wrangler jeans and Stetson hat. Outsiders who pegged him as a real-life J.R. Ewing couldn't have been more wrong. Carter was compassionate, not cutthroat. A real rags-to-riches success, he never forgot what it was like when he had nothing and how jealous he'd been of those with everything.

Carter was the son of a divorced mother who worked by day and went to school at night. At a young age, he went to work, too, delivering newspapers, pumping gas, selling french fries on the midway of the State Fair and hawking peanuts and programs at the Cotton Bowl and Moody Coliseum. That was about as close to sports as he got. If he had a sports hero, it was stunt driver Joey Chitwood. Young Donnie Joe's passions were hot rods and motorcycles, and several times they nearly got him killed.

His mother, the late Mary Crowley, wrote in her autobiography that she often said this prayer: "Lord, I know Don is going to do something great—please make it legal."

Carter dropped out of Crozier Tech High and joined the air force. Over the next four years, Mrs. C—as Carter called his mother—saw her prayers starting to be answered.

Carter finished his high school degree and became a devout Christian. Drinking and swearing were out. The straight and narrow were in. He worked at IBM, then joined his mother at Home Interiors & Gifts, the company she started in 1957 with a $6,000 bank loan. The company sold knick-knacks through direct sales. It caught on quickly, posting its first million-dollar year in 1962, and just kept growing.

In the early days of the business, Don met his future wife, Linda. She was only a year removed from playing basketball at Duncanville High, and several of their first dates were at a tournament there. For many years, the only picture in his wallet showed her in a basketball uniform.

Carter and his mother, who died of cancer in June 1986, were very involved in Christian causes. They were loyal followers of Billy Graham and big donors to the Fellowship of Christian Athletes; through that organization, the family became close with

Tom Landry and his family. Carter looked to Landry and the Cowboys when he started the Mavericks. He said he'd like to have "a team of Roger Staubachs." The clean-cut approach was symbolized by the first free agent signee: Ralph Drollinger, who came from the Christian-based Athletes in Action touring team.

Motta once said Carter was "too honest," adding that it would make a fine epitaph. Carter couldn't help it. He considered his favorite players almost like sons, sometimes crying when they were traded or released. When Oliver Mack was cut three days before Christmas 1981, Carter gave him a $3,000 going-away gift.

Carter went from rebelling against guaranteed contracts to being too generous with them. He was so loyal that sometimes his heart overtook his head, prompting him to overrule his basketball decision makers. He backed out of a fabulous deal with the Lakers because he didn't want the owner of his team's biggest rival to upset his general manager. Soon after, Carter took Mark Aguirre off the trading block because Aguirre's mother had died and Carter felt Aguirre needed stability in his life.

Carter was so forgiving of Roy Tarpley's problems with drugs and the law that he was criticized for sticking by Tarpley only because he was a great player. In response, team public relations director Kevin Sullivan asked Carter to let him tell the story of David Burns.

A Dallas native who starred at Saint Louis University, Burns played nine games for Denver in 1981-82, then tried making the Mavericks. He didn't and years later wound up working for Home Interiors & Gifts. When Carter discovered that Burns couldn't read, he personally made sure Burns got into an adult literacy program. Carter did it simply to help, not for attention, and only let Sullivan share the story to counter the bashing he was taking over Tarpley.

Another story Carter reluctantly let Sullivan tell involved four baseline seats he gave away to every home game. Carter paid for the tickets and wanted them given to people who would probably never get to sit so close to the action. So for several seasons in the 1990s, Carter had Sullivan or his top lieutenant, Tony Fay, roam the upper deck before each game in search of a lucky four-some. You can imagine the reactions they got. Sullivan and Fay still consider it a highlight of their Mavericks days.

"Some people say that a big heart doesn't fit in this business, but I've never been willing to accept that," Carter said in 1994.

Carter's relationship with fans was sealed on the day of the first game, when he told them, "We'll be contenders in three years."

While the rest of the basketball world laughed, he ended up being right.

NORM SONJU, GM

Until 1976, the man so responsible for bringing the NBA to Dallas had no connection to the league or the city. Norm Sonju's closest link was owning season tickets to the Chicago Bulls.

Then his friend Jerry Colangelo, who ran the Phoenix Suns, recommended him as a GM candidate to Buffalo Braves owner John Y. Brown. Sonju gave up a successful, lucrative business job to take it, then quickly discovered that Buffalo fans weren't inter-ested in the NBA. So Sonju began looking for somewhere to move the team. Dallas intrigued him partly because a new arena was being built and it lacked a pro sports tenant. He also liked California's Orange County, but it had no arena.

While some saw Dallas as a bastion for football and nothing else, Sonju noticed that TV ratings for NBA games were higher in Dallas than any other city without a team—and higher than some cities that did have a team.

Everything seemed to fall into place. In fact, Sonju was so sure the Braves were moving to Dallas that he bought a house, leased office space and negotiated a 20-year arena lease. He even decided to rename the team the Dallas Express.

Then Brown stunned Sonju by swapping his franchise for the Boston Celtics. The Braves' new owner moved the team to San Diego, where they became the Clippers.

After hooking up with Carter and getting a team in Dallas after all, Sonju was the first and only GM for 15 seasons. He later added titles such as chief operating officer and president. He also joined the league's expansion committee, the same group he once battled to get the rights for the Mavericks.

While opinions about him and his leadership style vary, the results speak for themselves. Dallas was labeled a "model" franchise in its first decade and often hosted people looking to start or rebuild teams.

Anyone who enjoyed a Mavericks game during his tenure can thank Sonju for pretty much everything except whatever happened on the court. Game-day operations were his forte, and he was a stickler for details. He took pride in everything from entertaining halftime shows to toilets that flushed and the temperature of food and drinks. Anyone who called his weekly radio show and complained about a squeaky chair would find it fixed by their next visit.

Optimism was one of Sonju's trademarks. A perfect illustration was his plan to cap season ticket sales at 14,000 to ensure that fans would always be able to buy single-game tickets. It seemed silly at the time, because Dallas averaged 7,789 fans the first season and there were still doubts about whether the NBA would catch on locally. Nobody was laughing about the ticket limit by the fourth season, when the average attendance hit 14,223.

Sonju's relationship with Colangelo and other NBA executives came through Camp of the Woods, a Christian camp in the Adirondack Mountains region of New York that Sonju became involved with as a teenager. Sonju and longtime NBA exec Pat Williams became so close through the camp that Williams was Sonju's best man. Don Nelson also was part of Sonju's wedding party. When Dallas hosted the 1986 All-Star Game, Sonju bought the court and donated it to the camp.

Sonju was such a devout Christian that "God Bless America" was played at home games instead of the national anthem.

While stories about his religion and tales regarding his idiosyncrasies—such as a crusade against Scotch tape—are how outsiders may remember Sonju, front office employees have mostly fond memories. They recall him everything from his Monday staff meetings to the annual Christmas party he hosted. He was also known to help anyone going through a tough time.

The Mavericks developed a family atmosphere few pro teams can match. Ask anyone who was involved back then what it was like, and their face lights up. Those warm, fuzzy feelings are shared by the team's first stars, too. Brad Davis and Rolando Blackman, the only two players whose jerseys have been retired, still work for the team. So does Derek Harper, another of the team's greatest players. Motta returned for a second stint as head coach seven years after his bitter departure. Even Aguirre and Tarpley were welcomed back after leaving on bad terms.

Sonju's relationship with Motta was never buddy-buddy, which may have factored into the coach's abrupt resignation in 1987. And Sonju was blamed for many bad decisions, most notably losing Sam Perkins to the Lakers. He also took heat in 1993 for saying during the prolonged negotiations with draft pick Jim Jackson that "it might be better to consider this our Lenny Bias," a reference to the Boston Celtics' top pick in 1986 who died of a cocaine overdose the day after the draft.

When Carter sold the team to a group led by Ross Perot Jr., Sonju remained, saying he was "glad to be part of the new future." But after two messy weeks, including the botched pursuit of Larry Brown to be the next coach, Sonju retired May 16, 1996.

"It's hard to believe I came here in February 1979 ... It's been extremely rewarding," he said when he left. "It's extremely, extremely disappointing that our team didn't nearly perform to the level we expected the last few years. But the pieces are in place now, and ... it's going to be fun again."

RICK SUND, BOY WONDER

Don Carter provided the money. Norm Sonju brought the front office savvy. But it was a young, unknown talent evaluator named Rick Sund who helped the Mavericks become so good, so fast.

Sund broke into the league in 1974 as an intern with the Milwaukee Bucks. There was plenty to do and few people to do it—a perfect opportunity for someone young and eager. Sund scouted college players, compiled statistics and helped break down game tapes with GM Wayne Embry and coach Don Nelson. He even got to lace 'em up occasionally and practice with the team. Sund could hold his own, too, having played basketball and football at Northwestern. After his senior year, the Bucks offered him a tryout, but he turned it down to attend graduate school.

When Sonju was getting the Dallas team ready, his pal Nelson recommended Sund. But Sonju wanted someone with more experience. Then Sund called Sonju and said he was going to be in the area and was hoping they could meet. It was a lie, but it worked. He got the interview and the job, becoming the league's youngest personnel director.

Sund got to do for real what thousands of 28-year-olds do now in fantasy leagues: build an NBA team from scratch. He made his mark in 1980 by milking a relationship with the Cleveland Cavaliers. Three trades involving marginal players yielded four first-round picks. He then turned those picks into Derek Harper, Sam Perkins, Detlef Schrempf and Roy Tarpley.

Sticking with a plan to build with youth, the Mavericks made the playoffs in four years and reached the Western Conference finals in 1988. That team's roster featured 10 Sund draft picks (nine first-rounders); the others were Brad Davis, whom Sund signed off the NBA's scrap heap during the first season, and James Donaldson, who came over in a trade and blossomed from journeyman to All-Star.

Sure, Sund had his share of mistakes. The names Bill Garnett, Terence Stansbury, Uwe Blab and Jim Farmer still make some fans cringe. Don't even mention Randy White, who was supposed to be the "next Mailman" after Dallas bypassed the original, Karl Malone.

For more than a decade, though, the good moves far outweighed the bad. Then he abandoned his original blueprint and brought in aging veterans Fat Lever, Rodney McCray and Alex English. While it made sense at the time—even sparking talk of a championship—hindsight shows it was a huge mistake. The final error was hiring Quinn Buckner. It eventually got Sund fired on April 12, 1994.

"I consider myself extremely lucky," he said that day. "I've been with one team for 14 seasons and 15 years. That's virtually unheard of."

Sund didn't exactly leave the place a mess. Dallas had seven first-round picks in the next four years, and Jamal Mashburn and Jim Jackson already were on the roster.

COACH MOTTA

The people running the pro basketball team in Dallas were looking for a coach, so they flew in Dick Motta for an interview. It was the early 1970s, and Motta was coaching the Chicago Bulls. The team was the Dallas Chaparrals of the American Basketball Association.

Motta turned it down, but was intrigued by the city. When he heard the Buffalo Braves were considering moving there, Motta said Dallas deserved better than someone else's leftovers. He recommended that Dallas get an expansion team.

At the time, Motta was coaching the Washington Bullets. He led them to the NBA championship in 1978 and returned to the finals in 1979. But he didn't think the team could do it again, so the next season he was ready to leave. He told the owner the team needed to be rebuilt and that he wasn't interested in doing it. Rumors started that what Motta really wanted was to help start the expansion team in Dallas, which was close to becoming a reality.

Motta got one of the first interviews. But Sonju wasn't impressed.

"His chances of getting the job are zero," said Sonju, who owned Bulls season tickets when Motta was the coach.

Sonju's top choice, Eddie Sutton of Arkansas, didn't want the job. Larry Brown wasn't ready to leave UCLA. By July, the front-runner was Bob Weiss, a former Motta player who was now a Clippers assistant. But Carter wanted a proven commodity. Like Motta. So Carter told Sonju to set up another interview, this time on Motta's turf.

When Carter's private jet arrived at a former air force base near Motta's off-season hometown—Fish Haven, Idaho—the coach thought the guy who walked out wearing jeans and a cowboy hat was the pilot. Nope, that was Mr. C. The two bonded quickly over fried chicken. Sitting on beanbags in the back of a pickup truck, Motta told Carter he wanted the job. Carter told him it was his.

"It was a different Dick Motta than the one I had talked to in May," Sonju said. "He didn't sound tired or bored. He sounded like a man who wanted to coach in the NBA."

Motta grew up on a farm in Midvale, Utah. The primary influence in his life was his father, an Italian immigrant who worked the copper mines. Motta knew from a young age that he wanted to be a coach—good thing, because at 5-foot-8 he wasn't going to have much of a playing career. He was cut from the varsity high school basketball team his senior season and never made his college team at Utah State despite trying out all four years. Instead, he became a conference champion wrestler.

His first coaching job was at a junior high in Grace, Idaho, in 1953. He led the seventh graders to the championship game, then spent two years in the air force. He returned to Grace in the fall of '56 as the high school coach. The kids from his old squad were now sophomores. As seniors, they won the state title. One of the players was Phil Johnson, who would become a Motta assistant in college and the pros and eventually win NBA Coach of the Year.

From Grace, Motta moved up to Weber Junior College, where his first team went 17-8. The next year, the school became Weber State, a four-year university. Despite the upgrade to Division I, the team improved to 22-4 and went on to win three of the first four Big Sky Conference titles.

Motta's success convinced the upstart Chicago Bulls to give him a try. They were quite a pair: Motta had never seen an NBA game before coaching one, and the Bulls had gone 62-101 in their first two seasons.

Motta was a my-way-or-the-highway kind of coach. He'd been taught the importance of respecting authority by his father and demanded it from his players. He ranted and raved often—kicking balls, slamming chairs and screaming at players and referees. He became the first NBA coach suspended for a week.

What his Bulls teams lacked in talent they made up for with grit and hard work. That was epitomized by Jerry Sloan, who never saw a loose ball that wasn't worth diving for or a charge not worth taking. Motta got the most out of his "blue-collar" teams by implementing an offense with lots of passes and picks, and he taught them to be opportunistic on defense.

Chicago went 51-31 in his third season, and he was named Coach of the Year. They had 57, 54 and 51 wins the next three years, but struggled in the playoffs.

Two years later, Motta took over in Washington. The Bullets had stars like Elvin Hayes and Wes Unseld, but needed a strong leader. In Motta's second season, Washington beat Dr. J and the heavily favored Philadelphia 76ers in the conference finals, then trailed Seattle 3-2 in the NBA Finals. That's when Motta entered a phrase into sports lore.

"The opera ain't over until the fat lady sings," he said.

Although Motta admittedly borrowed the line from San Antonio scribe Dan Cook, it was the coach—and his timing—who helped popularize it. Washington rallied to win the series and got to celebrate in style. The Bullets received the keys to the city, met with President Carter at the White House, and were honored with a motorcade down Pennsylvania Avenue.

That was June 1978. In July 1980, Motta was at the Hyatt Regency hotel in Dallas being introduced as the first coach of the Mavericks.

"I hope we have enough energy to get the fat lady out of the mire," he said. "Someday she'll sing in Dallas. I can guarantee that."

BEFORE THE MAVS, DALLAS HAD THE CHAPS

The first professional basketball team in Dallas was the Chaparrals of the American Basketball Association. They began in 1967 with 30 owners who knew each other mostly through Southern Methodist University and business deals. The nickname came from the hotel ballroom where the team held meetings.

The first draft provided an ominous start. Franchise holder Roland Speth had a list of prospects that he assumed was in order of preference. Imagine how excited he was at getting his first five choices. Then he discovered that the list was in alphabetical order.

The Chaps never captured the city's heart. Their fan base was only around 2,500, and the biggest crowd was 7,800. They tried pumping up interest by taking the 1970-71 team on the road, even renaming themselves the Texas Chaparrals. They returned to Dallas the next season.

Besides stars like Julius Erving and Moses Malone, the ABA was filled with players the NBA didn't want. The Chaps had their share, including a hotshot who played with a toothpick in his mouth.

Although the Chaps made the playoffs five times in six seasons, rising costs and plummeting interest took a toll. In 1973, a group of out-of-town businessmen led by car dealer Red McCombs and Angelo Drossos leased the team and moved it to their hometown, with the understanding that if all went well they would buy the club.

You'd have to say things worked out. Renamed the San Antonio Spurs, they were among four ABA teams allowed to join the NBA in the 1976 merger. In 1999, they became the first ex-ABA team to win an NBA title. In 2003, they beat the Mavericks in the Western Conference finals and went on to win their second championship.

The failed hoops experiment didn't sour one part-owner—Robert Folsom, who as Dallas mayor played a key role in luring the NBA. Another Chaps part-owner was Lindsey Embrey. He was one of seven who lasted till the end, then was one of six original minority partners in the Mavericks. He still owns a chunk of the team.

REUNION ARENA

The flat-topped, glassy building at 777 Sports Street was hailed as state of the art when it was built for $27 million. The project was pushed through by Mayor Folsom, who never even gave taxpayers the chance to say no.

Folsom—a former four-sport letterman at SMU who had been president of the school board and a successful realtor and developer—avoided a public vote by finding a unique way to fund the project.

The plan was to sell revenue bonds and individual bonds to season ticket holders. The city council approved it in November 1977 and ground was broken March 15, 1978. Critics—and there were plenty—thought Folsom had pulled a fast one. They ridiculed the building as "Folsom's Folly" and "The House That Bobby Built." A popular joke was that it was built next to a train station because the project had been railroaded. The backlash was so strong that when voters were offered a bond proposition to pay for a street system around the facility, they rejected it.

But once Reunion opened, it drew rave reviews.

"Two years after it opened, it was the most successful building the city owned," Folsom bragged.

As the Mavericks became contenders, the atmosphere inside became electric. Fans were proudly known as "Reunion Rowdies."

*Reunion Arena was the star of the 1986 All-Star Game,
but without luxury suites, it became obsolete by the late 1990s.*

"It was one of the loudest buildings I ever played in," said former Mavericks star Brad Davis, whose jersey later hung from the rafters. "It got so loud sometimes that you couldn't even hear yourself think."

Reunion was among the last major sports venues built without money-generating luxury boxes. They actually had been in the original plans, following the lead of trendsetting Texas Stadium in nearby Irving.

Over 21 seasons, the Mavs went 428-417 in Reunion. Many media events were held in "The Folsom Room," where a framed portrait of its namesake still hangs facing the room's main entrance.

2

The Expansion Season

THE NICKNAME AND LOGO

Approximately two months before Dallas received a franchise, nominations were taken for a nickname. WBAP-AM, the team's first and longtime radio home, collected 4,600 entries in three weeks. Among them were Armadillos, Derricks, Dollars, Goatheads, Hoop 'N' Cranes, Millionaires and Snail Darters.

The finalists were Express, Wranglers, and Mavericks. Sonju and Carter liked Mavericks, but the University of Texas-Arlington already used it. The team tried smoothing things out with the school, even noting that their basketball team was known as the Movin' Mavs, not Mavericks. Some hard feelings lingered, though. A popular bumper sticker in 1980 read "Mavericks Nowhere But UTA." For what it's worth, the team had an unwritten rule against using "Mavs" throughout Sonju's tenure.

The logo underwent 77 revisions before it was unveiled. The italicized M was meant to depict movement. Blue and green were chosen for the colors because they represented a "North Texas countryside scheme," Sonju said.

THE DISPERSAL DRAFT, CLEVELAND FLEECING

The strategy in a dispersal draft is the reverse of a college draft. Instead of obtaining the best players, teams try avoiding the worst ones. In choosing from the four least wanted players from all 22 teams, the Mavericks could've gone for some big-name players to try selling tickets. Pete Maravich, Earl Monroe and Spencer Haywood were all available.

But they focused on younger players. They took 15 guys who'd been in the league two seasons or less and four more who'd been around three or four years. Sonju chose this path after talking to officials with the Utah Jazz, the last expansion team stocked through a dispersal draft.

"They went for big names, lost their draft choices, and they are still paying for their mistakes," Sonju said soon after.

Only 11 of the picks ever played for the Mavericks. Just two made it past the first season: Tom LaGarde (two seasons) and Jim Spanarkel (four). The other nine played a combined 282 games. But the Mavericks often got the most out of them.

They started small, sending Wiley Peck to Phoenix for a second-round pick in 1981, then shipping Billy McKinney to Utah for a second-rounder in '83. Then came the smartest move—calling Cleveland. The Mavs and Cavs made three separate trades, starting with Mike Bratz for a first-round pick in 1984. Then Richard Washington and Jerome Whitehead went north in exchange for a first-rounder in 1983 (which Cleveland had gotten from Atlanta), a first-rounder in '86, and Bill Robinzine.

With other teams crying out against the deals, the league declared that it would have to approve any future Cleveland trades. That didn't stop Rick Sund from swapping Geoff Huston and a 1983 third-rounder for a first-rounder in '85 and Chad Kinch. What helped "balance" this deal was the fact that Huston was Dallas's leading scorer at 16.1 points per game. Most of the complaints were about what Cleveland was doing. Coach Bill Musselman was willing to mortgage the future to save his job now, and owner Ted Stepian let him do it.

Some said the Mavericks were making a mistake by trading their best, most marketable players with no guarantee of getting anything better. Outsiders warned that the NBA wouldn't survive in Dallas if the moves backfired. The Mavericks, though, loved the idea of 10 first-round picks in the next six drafts.

"What if we hit on five of them? What if we ... hit on all of them?" coach Dick Motta said after the final Cleveland trade. "Realize how quickly a team can be built with the correct approach."

The Mavericks turned those extra picks into Derek Harper, Sam Perkins, Detlef Schrempf and Roy Tarpley, all of whom would play key roles in the team's rise. Motta would later say that Sund "ought to be arrested for" having stolen such talent from Cleveland. The NBA police eventually arrived on the scene to prevent teams from trading first-round picks in consecutive drafts. It's known as either the "Stepien Rule" or the "Sund Rule."

After Stepien sold the Cavaliers in May 1983—ending a three-year reign of error—the league took mercy on the new owners and restored first-round picks from '83-86. (Imagine trying something like that now!)

If you're wondering why Stepien didn't give Dallas the first pick in '82, it's because he couldn't. Cleveland's previous owners traded it to Los Angeles for a forgettable player named Don Ford. The Lakers turned that pick into James Worthy.

THE FIRST DRAFT: THE KIKI CHRONICLES

With the first pick in team history, the Mavericks selected a guy who didn't want to be in Dallas and already had told them so. His name was Kiki Vandeweghe, although for the next six months he was called a lot of unprintable things.

Vandeweghe was a two-time All-American who had helped UCLA play for the NCAA title that year. He was represented by his father, Ernie, himself a former NBA player. They told Dallas that Kiki only wanted to play for the New York Knicks (who had the pick right after Dallas) or the Los Angeles Lakers (who didn't have a first-rounder).

Sonju called the Knicks and asked if they wanted to switch picks, but they said no. So the Mavericks—picking 11th—took Vandeweghe anyway. Vandeweghe repeated his stance in a conference call with reporters immediately after the draft. Three months into the stalemate, he said: "I'm sorry it came to this. I want to be near my family and friends. I've made that clear from the beginning."

In December, the Mavs traded Vandeweghe's rights to Denver for the Nuggets' top pick the following season. That became the ninth pick, a slight upgrade. Dallas used it on a guy named Rolando Blackman. Maybe you've heard of him—he's the leading scorer in team history.

"It turned out to be a good thing for everyone involved," said Vandeweghe, who became a two-time All-Star and reached the playoffs in 12 of his 13 seasons with Denver, Portland, New York and the Los Angeles Clippers. He retired in 1993 with a career average of 19.7 points.

Dallas fans held a first-class grudge against Vandeweghe throughout his career. Whenever he played in Reunion Arena, boos drowned the introduction of his name and echoed again every time he had the ball. He eventually looked forward to it. But he wasn't ready the first time—December 26, 1980, just a few weeks into his career. Fans brought signs like "Daddy, Can I Shoot Now?" and "Key-Key Please Call Home—Daddy." Vandeweghe went two for eight, scoring eight points in a 119-111 Denver loss that gave Dallas just its fifth win.

"It's nice that people care," Vandeweghe said after the game.

Vandeweghe's stance against Dallas eventually softened. When he signed a contract later in his career, he listed the Mavericks among five teams to which he could be traded.

Still, the saga has a more surprising postscript. Vandeweghe was hired by Dallas in 1999 as a part-time assistant working with the team's big men. A year later, he became a full-time assistant and director of player development. The year after that,

Vandeweghe returned to Denver as general manager and swung a huge trade that sent Raef LaFrentz and Nick Van Exel to the Mavericks. Vandeweghe later tried hiring two Dallas assistants as his coach, but both said no. Mavs fans with long memories had to smile at the snub.

THE REST OF THE FIRST DRAFT CLASS

Darrrell Allums was the only member of the original draft class who made the opening day roster. Allums, who went to UCLA with Vandeweghe, was taken in the fifth round. He played only 22 games, then was waived in January 1981.

The "most distinguished" member of the 1980 crop ended up being eighth-rounder Clarence Kea. Despite being cut during the first, second and third training camps, Kea was brought back for a total of 51 games. After being dropped the first time, Kea worked in a guitar factory in Bethlehem, Pennsylvania. But what makes him even more memorable was his shoe size: 18 EEE.

WE HARDLY KNEW YA

In 23 seasons, more than 150 players have suited up for the Dallas Mavericks.

Some didn't last very long.

Monti Davis is the patriarch of this group. Signed to a 10-day contract on January 2, 1981, that's all he lasted. He played eight minutes in one game, scoring a single point. He actually shot five free throws—one of them an air ball.

Davis happened to be with the Mavericks when the inaugural team photo was taken. Coaches already knew they were going to waive Davis when his deal expired, so he was kindly asked not to get into the picture. That's why there are only 11 players in the first team photo.

A roster spot had opened for Davis when Ralph Drollinger—the team's first free agent signee—went on the injured list with a knee problem that forced him to retire ... after just six games.

So in honor of Davis and Drollinger, here's everyone who played six games or less for the Mavericks, listed in order of appearance:

Name	Game(s)	Season
Mark Wade	1	1989-90
Howard Wright	3	1990-91
Joao Vianna	1	1991-92
Tom Garrick	6	1991-92
Chucky Brown	1	1993-94
(Brown never missed a shot, going one for one from the field and the foul line.)		
Reggie Slater	3	1995-96
Jason Sasser	2	1996-97
Stacey King	6	1996-97
Adrian Caldwell	1	1997-98
Kurt Thomas	5	1997-98
Randell Jackson	1	1999-00
(Jackson played just one minute. The rest of his stat line was all zeroes.)		
Rodrick Rhodes	1	1999-00
Bill Curley	5	2000-01
Obinna Ekezie	4	2000-01
Darrick Martin	3	2001-02
Charlie Bell	2	2001-02

Two more unique stories involve John Hollinden and Jimmy Lampley, two draftees who never made the roster.

The fact that Hollinden stood 7-foot-6 was reason enough for Dallas to draft him with the 185th pick of the 1981 draft. He played college ball at Indiana State-Evansville, but obviously not very well or else he wouldn't have been available in the ninth round.

Lampley was a 6-foot-10 center taken in the fifth round of the 1983 draft. He came to camp overweight, and coach Dick

Motta cut him one day into training camp while preparing for a workout.

"I've never cut a guy during stretching exercises before," Motta said.

GETTING CLOSER

A series of "firsts" preceded the true debut of the Mavericks. They include:

**First workout, September 8, 1980. Seven rookies and seven veterans practiced at Royal Haven Baptist Church on a court that wasn't even the full NBA length. Training camp opened five days later with a crew Motta described as "basically four types of people: People with bad contracts, people with a bad injury, people with a bad attitude or a bad player. Some of them qualified for three of the four categories."

** First preseason game, September 20. Playing at the Lloyd Noble Center on the University of Oklahoma campus, Dallas beat the Denver Nuggets 122-98. The game was also noteworthy because it was the team's first game that was broadcast on radio—but only in Denver, not Dallas. The real twist is that it was called by Mark Holtz, who already had been hired as the first voice of the Mavericks. While basketball brought Holtz to Dallas, he became a local icon for his work with baseball's Texas Rangers.

** First home preseason game, September 26. Dallas lost to Philadelphia 113-108 in front of 15,634 fans at Reunion Arena, including NBA commissioner Larry O'Brien. Dallas played the nightcap of a preseason doubleheader marking the first two games played at Reunion Arena. Houston beat Kansas City 128-106 in the opener.

FIRST GAME EQUALS FIRST WIN

The first regular-season game the Mavericks ever played wasn't even the biggest sporting event in town that day. NBA schedule makers failed to realize—or possibly just didn't care—that the second Saturday in October is when Texas and Oklahoma renew their annual football rivalry at the Cotton Bowl. On October 11, 1980, the Longhorns were No. 3 in the country and the Sooners were No. 12. Texas won 20-13, and some fans made their way from Fair Park to Reunion Arena a few hours later for the historic NBA game.

Before a crowd of 10,373—which was considered big—the Mavericks pulled off a stunning 103-92 victory over the San Antonio Spurs, the franchise that began a few miles away as the Dallas Chaparrals. (Give the schedule makers credit for getting that part right.)

The new Dallas team debuted with a starting lineup of Winford Boynes, Geoff Huston, Tom LaGarde, Abdul Jeelani and Jerome Whitehead. Boynes scored a team-high 21 points, and LaGarde grabbed 14 rebounds. Fans who feared a typical expansion season (in other words, a disaster) were now dreaming of 82-0.

"I'm going to enjoy this today," coach Dick Motta said. "I'm not going to look too far ahead. I'm just going to follow the tall guys."

While Spurs coach Stan Albeck gave the backhanded compliment of saying the Mavericks "will not finish last in the NBA," star player George Gervin gave Dallas far less credit.

"New kids don't last long in a man's world," said Gervin, who scored 22 points in the first half, but only 11 in the second half. "It won't be like this next time."

It wasn't. The Mavericks followed their successful debut by losing the next five, 15 of the next 16 and 27 of the next 29. The Spurs went on to win the Midwest Division, beating the Mavericks all five times they met later that season. But for one day, the Mavericks were unbeaten. An autographed ball from that game remains on display in Carter's office.

BRAD DAVIS ARRIVES

Other than the Cleveland deals, the next best thing Rick Sund did during 1980-81 was fly to Montana to scout Ronnie Valentine. Who, you ask? Valentine was a 6-foot-7 forward who was the last cut in Denver's training camp. He wound up with the Montana Golden Nuggets of the CBA, and his coach, George Karl, urged Sund to give the kid a look. So Sund flew out for a November 28 game against the Anchorage Northern Knights.

Valentine was OK. Sund, though, was more impressed by Anchorage point guard Brad Davis. A former All-American at Maryland, Davis had left college early and had failed to catch on in the NBA. He'd played for—in order—the Lakers, the World Basketball Association's Montana Sky, the Indiana Pacers, Anchorage, and the Utah Jazz. Davis had started that season in training camp with the Detroit Pistons, but was cut the day before the opener.

It was too late to enroll in college, so Davis made plans to attend Cal State-Northridge in the spring. Anchorage invited him back, and he eventually decided to go merely to finish out his basketball career. He was so serious about quitting that he even turned down a chance to leave Alaska and join the Kansas City Kings.

Then Sund spotted him. Sund told Motta what he'd seen, and the coach said he'd take him. But Davis wasn't interested. He told Sund that. Twice. However, Davis's business manager encouraged him to go, as did Mavericks assistant coach Bob Weiss. Weiss told Davis his own tale of blossoming in Motta's system after being rescued from the minors. Dallas even offered the equivalent of two 10-day contracts so that he could leave before Christmas and resume his college education. Davis finally said yes, signing on December 2.

Standing out with blond, curly hair and a mustache, Davis immediately convinced coaches that he was better than incumbent point guard Geoff Huston. So Sund dealt his leading scorer to Cleveland. And Davis decided to stay. His breakout perfor-

*Brad Davis's all-out playing style made him so beloved by
fans that his No. 15 became the first jersey retired by the team.
(NBAE/Getty Images)*

mance came March 3 in a 117-105 loss to eventual NBA champion Boston. He made 14 of 17 shots—including 11 in a row—and scored 31 points, the most yet by a Dallas player. He also had 13 assists and five rebounds.

By the mid-1980s, Davis was the last member of the initial team still in Dallas. To make it, he had to fight off many challenges for his job, first as a starter and then as a reserve. He outlasted the near-drafting of Isiah Thomas, the acquisition of Kelvin Ransey and the arrival of Derek Harper. He eventually made a smooth transition in handing his starting job over to Harper, who later praised his pal as one of the smartest point guards he'd ever seen. Davis always played as if he feared getting cut. That attitude produced an energetic style that made him loved by teammates, coaches and fans.

When he retired after the 1991-92 season, Davis was the team leader in games (883), consecutive games (246), assists (4,524), personal fouls (2,040) and consecutive three-pointers (10). He also won the Favorite Maverick Award in five of the franchise's first six seasons.

He received a long standing ovation before his final home game in April 1992. Seven months later, at the urging of fans, the team made his No. 15 jersey the first to be retired.

"I'm very overwhelmed," Davis said during an emotional 20-minute ceremony. "You've made my 12 years here the happiest of my life."

Davis still hasn't left the club, working as an assistant coach and on the team's radio and television crews.

"I guess it's a good thing for us that Montana played Anchorage that night," Sund said.

GARY COLE, aka ABDUL JEELANI, aka MR. FOURTH QUARTER

Abdul Jeelani scored the first points in team history with an 18-foot jumper against San Antonio. But he's best known for three incredible fourth quarters.

It started December 26, 1980, when he upstaged the "home-coming" of Kiki Vandeweghe. Jeelani entered at the start of the final period and scored 20 points, leading Dallas to a 119-111 victory. The crowd got so into it that they screamed "Abdul! Abdul! Abdul!" a bizarre sound from a gathering of mostly white, twangy Texans.

The Mavericks wouldn't win again until January 13, 1981, when Jeelani scored all 16 of his points in the fourth, carrying Dallas past the Chicago Bulls 112-106. Adding to the drama was the fact that Jeelani had been out with back spasms. He played slathered in salve and fitted with a rubber corset.

"I'm not going to let Abdul practice any more," Motta said. "He's been lying on the training table for four days, and I've been mad at him. I know he won't play before the fourth quarter again."

Bill Robinzine joked that he and LaGarde deserved most of the credit.

"Tommy and I go in there and wear them down for three quarters, get them so tired they can't walk, then he comes in and milks them," Robinzine said. "Is that fair?"

Jeelani did it again three nights later, personally outscoring the Knicks 21-20 in the final period of a 118-110 victory. It marked the first time Dallas ever won consecutive games and the first time the Mavericks won when trailing after three quarters.

Motta actually turned to his fourth-quarter specialist a little early, giving him six third-quarter minutes. Jeelani missed both his shots that period, then went eight for 10 in the fourth. Jim Spanarkel and Winford Boynes watched in awe from the bench. After his first few baskets, they were already predicting he'd score 20.

"He came off the floor with a scratch on his arm," Spanarkel said. "I was glad to see him bleed blood. I was glad to see he didn't bleed three-point goals and turnaround jumpers."

Jeelani, who was known as Gary Cole until becoming a Muslim in the late 1970s, had arrived in Dallas with the typical resume of a dispersal draft pick. At 26, he'd been cut by two teams and not protected by a third. He had a reputation for getting out of control on offense, his best seasons were overseas, and he was coming off knee surgery.

After the season, Dallas waived Jeelani at his request so that he could play in Italy.

EXPANSION MOMENTS

What would an expansion season be without wacky moments? These are some of the best.

October 15, 1980, vs. Denver

Ah, the first road game. A first-class affair, right? Not even close. Although a bus was chartered to take the team from the airport to the hotel, there was no driver. So after waiting 20 minutes, everyone piled into four cabs.

The driver caught up to the team at the hotel. When assistant coach Bob Weiss asked about his absence at the airport, the driver said he was there, "But I didn't see anyone who looked like a basketball player."

Neither did the Nuggets. They beat Dallas 133-98.

October 25, 1980, vs. Golden State

Motta sent a message players would never forget by bringing a tiger into the locker room. The animal was at the arena in Oakland to perform with a chimpanzee at halftime of a game against Golden State. In what could be a story all its own, the chimp made more baskets during halftime than Dallas did in the first two quarters.

Motta arranged for the trainer to bring him the tiger after the show. Holding the animal by its leash, Motta walked in and announced, "If you guys don't start rebounding, I'm going to let this tiger eat."

He certainly got the attention of Jeelani, who jumped on a training table.

The Mavericks lost anyway.

October 31, 1980, vs. Utah

It was called the "Halloween Massacre." The Mavericks were crushed 144-122 by the Utah Jazz in Salt Lake City. Four players fouled out, and Adrian Dantley scored 50 points, still the most by an opponent in regulation.

November 8, 1980, vs. Detroit

The 16th game in Mavericks history was the 1,000th of Motta's career. He became only the fourth coach to reach that milestone. Motta celebrated by continuing his ongoing campaign to get officials to respect his ragtag team.

Early in the fourth quarter, official Tommy Nunez said enough is enough and ejected Motta. The Mavericks lost 101-73 to the Pistons.

Over his first two seasons, Motta got 48 technical fouls and was tossed seven times.

February 4, 1981, vs. Houston

Having lost six straight and playing the night after a 121-100 loss to the Kings, the Mavericks traveled to Houston for their worst letdown of the season. The Rockets thumped them 116-68, a low point total that would hold up as the team's worst for 16 seasons.

February 22, 1981, vs. New Jersey

Another blowout—only this time, there's a twist. Dallas won!

After losing a season-worst 15 straight games, the Mavericks took out their frustrations on the Nets, winning 132-109. It was their widest margin of victory.

February 27, 1981, vs. Indiana

Warning: This is not for anyone with a weak stomach. Actually, that was the problem during the second quarter of a game against Indiana.

Pacers forward George Johnson vomited near the top of the key, leaving a puddle that Dallas guard Oliver Mack slipped on during a fast break. Mack wiped out, and Indiana's Clemon Johnson was grossed out. Realizing what had happened, George Johnson fled the court—drawing a technical foul against the Pacers for not having enough players on the court.

Jim Spanarkel hit the technical free throw, but Dallas lost anyway 118-111.

"Who would do something like that on a court?" said Mack, who had 26 points on 13 of 23 shooting.

Indiana coach Jack McKinney jokingly credited George Johnson's defense.

"That was the only way we could stop Mack," McKinney said.

March 1, 1981, vs. San Diego

Playing in front of 4,858 fans, the smallest home crowd of the season, the Mavericks avoided the worst record in NBA history by winning their 10th game. It took 68 games, but Dallas finally guaranteed itself a better record than the 1972-73 Philadelphia 76ers with a 99-91 victory over the San Diego Clippers.

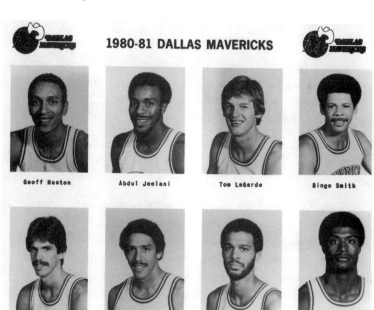

1980-81 DALLAS MAVERICKS

Geoff Huston   Abdul Jeelani   Tom LaGarde   Bingo Smith

Jim Spanarkel   Raymond Townsend   Richard Washington   Jerome Whitehead

Of these original Mavericks, LaGarde was an instant fan favorite, Jeelani became Mr. Fourth Quarter, Spanarkel lasted the longest, and Houston, Washington and Whitehead were traded to Cleveland. Smith and Townsend failed to make it out of training camp.
(NBAE/Getty Images)

"I really thought at the time that we had the worst team in the history of the NBA," Sund said. "But I didn't want us to finish with the worst record."

Sund was a 28-year-old personnel director trying to make a name for himself. Being attached to the "record loser" label wasn't the way, so it's understandable why he later listed this as his top memory of the team's first 10 seasons.

March 20, 1981, vs. Denver

After 76 games, it would've been understandable if players were more focused on summer vacation than basketball. But starting with a 126-125 win over Denver at home on March 20, the Mavericks won three of four—their best streak of the season. They couldn't keep it up, though, closing the season with two losses.

"This is the best group of pros I've ever worked with," Motta said after the second win in the streak, 105-95 victory over Utah on March 21. "I don't think in 20 years I'll be able to look back and say I've ever had a better bunch. None of you knew you belonged before this season started, and now that you do, you have a reason to be proud of yourself."

March 29, 1981, vs. Portland

Usually, the home team wows the crowd. This time, it was the other way around. At the Mavericks' home finale, a crowd of 11,203 gave the team a prolonged standing ovation during pre-game introductions. It was the ultimate sign that the team had been adopted and appreciated by the community. The team responded by standing and applauding the fans. That mutual admiration became a tradition at home finales for many seasons.

"I was covered with goose bumps," said center Scott Lloyd, who responded by scoring a career-high 28 points in a 123-109 loss to the Portland Trail Blazers.

Although the Mavericks sold out only two games that season—both against the Los Angeles Lakers—the average attendance of 7,789 was the best ever for an NBA expansion team.

It was likely that Dallas also sold a lot of programs that season, considering how quickly the roster turned over. There were a total of 21 players, with only Spanarkel and LaGarde playing every game.

The Mavericks finished 15-67 with losing streaks of 10, 12 and 15.

"We could have won more games had we kept veteran players and picked up others who've been offered," Motta said late in the inaugural season. "But where would we be next training camp?"

3

Mavs Take Off

1981 DRAFT—THE NO. 1 PICK AND THEN SOME

Dallas got the No. 1 pick in the 1981 draft when Detroit called heads and a coin came up tails.

The Mavericks debated between three can't-miss kids: small forward Mark Aguirre, point guard Isiah Thomas and power forward Buck Williams.

Aguirre was a go-to guy, a premier scorer who would fit perfectly into Motta's forward-driven system. Yet there were questions about his attitude.

Thomas was a playmaker, a prototype on-court leader who could find the open man or hit a shot himself. But Dallas already had a solid point guard in Brad Davis. Sure, Thomas was better, but the Mavericks needed to upgrade other spots and Davis was a coach and fan favorite. Thomas also didn't do so well when he came to town for an interview—although he later admitted he tanked on purpose.

Williams was a banger, a strong inside presence who would gobble up rebounds. He had great character, too. The knock was that he lacked the pizzazz to handle the hype of being a No. 1 pick.

Aguirre could be electrifying, either with post-up moves in the paint or by stretching defenses with his endless range. And he played a position Dallas needed to fill. So on June 8, 1981, the Mavericks made Aguirre the top choice.

But that pick was just the start. Dallas also had the No. 9 overall choice, courtesy of Denver and the Kiki Vandeweghe trade. Had Vandeweghe signed, the Mavericks would've had their small forward, so they wouldn't have needed Aguirre. And they wouldn't have had this pick—which was used on Rolando Blackman.

Dallas used the opening pick of the second round on Jay Vincent, a forward who had played alongside Magic Johnson at Michigan State. Still in the second round, Dallas also had the 43rd choice thanks to the first trade in team history. It yielded Elston Turner, a shooting guard who beat out Blackman for playing time during their rookie season.

Any team in any sport would love to have one draft class as good as this one.

FAN FRIENDLY

By inviting fans to Union Station to watch the 1981 draft, the Dallas Mavericks continued their strong relationship with a growing fan base.

The draft was more novelty than glitzy event back then. There weren't weeks of hype, draft gurus on TV and radio and entire magazines devoted to it. Yet it was important locally because Dallas was picking first. So the team threw a party, which it continued to do into the 1990s.

Training camp was another time fans and the team bonded. From 1981-92, fans were invited to Moody Coliseum to watch the evening session during two-a-day workouts. Mundane drills were livened by cheers, and fans got to meet the players. Coach Quinn Buckner stopped it in 1993 by training in Waco, but it was restarted in '94 when Dick Motta returned as coach.

In the mid-'90s, when things on the court were terrible, the team thanked season ticket holders with a party at Six Flags. The entire park was rented out, and Don Nelson was at the front greeting guests as they arrived.

AGUIRRE'S IMPACT

Donald Carter had a unique way of convincing Aguirre to be a team player. During a pre-draft visit to Dallas, Aguirre went to Carter's ranch, and the two went for a walk. Carter told Aguirre that whatever he'd done in the past was strictly in the past. If the Mavericks took him, he'd come in with a clean slate—and he'd better keep it clean.

If he didn't? Carter pointed to a stake "where we'd tie up horses when we were breaking them." He hinted that Aguirre could wind up chained to it if he broke that vow.

"It was a few years before he forgot the sight of that post," Carter said nearly a decade later.

Whatever the motivation, Aguirre started fast and relatively trouble-free. (Well, Motta did have to yell at him to speed up while running sprints on his first day of training camp.) Aguirre led the team in scoring and rebounding in his first game, then scored a team-record 42 points in his ninth game. He led the team in scoring in 10 of the first 12 games and was named Rookie of the Month for November.

On December 9, he learned that he had the most All-Star votes in the Western Conference. That night, he broke his foot while making a layup in Kansas City. He missed 31 games, ruining his chances of becoming an All-Star or Rookie of the Year.

Aguirre came back as a reserve because Motta was upset with his play and conditioning. Aguirre finished the season averaging 18.7 points, almost three behind Jay Vincent. It would be the last time Aguirre failed to lead the team in scoring until he was traded.

HE'S CALLED "BIG DADDY" FOR A REASON

When Aguirre went down, Jay "Big Daddy" Vincent stepped up. Vincent replaced Aguirre in the starting lineup and atop the stat sheet, averaging 24.9 points while making 50 percent of his shots the rest of the season. He came within a point of Aguirre's scoring record, going for 41 on December 29.

Vincent became the first Maverick named Player of the Week when he averaged 32.3 points and 7.3 rebounds while leading Dallas past Seattle and New Jersey in February. In the next game, he had 40 points and 10 rebounds in just three quarters. He led the team in points, minutes and steals, and finished third in Rookie of the Year voting behind—guess who?—Williams and Thomas.

"I can't imagine any player helping his team any more than Jay helped us," Motta said. "He just amazed me at times."

LAST-SECOND STUNT BACKFIRES

Down by two with one second left and Houston's Elvin Hayes about to shoot a free throw, Motta knew something drastic had to be done. So Motta told his big men to make sure the shot didn't go in.

Wayne Cooper did so with zeal, popping the ball into the second row. It was such a blatant move that officials decided to count the shot as a made basket—and gave another one for Cooper's unsportsmanlike conduct. Hayes made it, sealing a 99-95 victory.

"They said it was intentional," Motta said. "Can they read our minds?"

SIGNS OF PROGRESS

The 1981-82 season proved the Mavericks' plan was working. With big contributions from rookies, Dallas won 28 games, 13 more than the inaugural season.

The Mavs started 1-13 and were 4-16 when Aguirre got hurt. Then a victory on December 29 began a 12-15 stretch. There was even a four-game winning streak in that run, started by a 15-point comeback win over eventual division champion Milwaukee.

"Our team is a credit to the league in the way they play," Motta said during the streak. "I don't mean to sound corny, but they are."

Some of the best victories included an overtime win against the Rockets—despite league MVP Moses Malone scoring 44 points and grabbing 16 rebounds—and a win over the eventual league champion Lakers sealed by Aguirre hitting a three-pointer with seven seconds left in the game.

"We weren't necessarily looking for a three-pointer, but with Mark, it is the same as a 10-footer," Motta said.

The biggest change from the first season was that Dallas now wore green road uniforms. Superstition said it was the blue outfits that caused the Mavericks to go 4-37 away from home that first season. At the time, the Dallas Cowboys were said to be jinxed when they wore blue on the road. Wearing their everyday-is-St.-Patrick's-Day clothes, Dallas improved to 12-29 on the road.

TOO GOOD FOR THEIR OWN GOOD

The downside of the second-season success was having the fourth pick in the 1982 draft—a draft that was widely seen as having three elite players (James Worthy, Terry Cummings, and Dominique Wilkins), then everyone else. The Lakers took James Worthy. San Diego got Terry Cummings. Utah chose Dominique Wilkins.

The Mavericks went with Bill Garnett, whose contribution to team history is that he was the first major draft mistake. About the best thing that can be said of Garnett's career in Dallas was that he and another bad pick—Terence Stansbury—were eventually packaged to Indiana for a first-rounder.

Among the players the Mavericks considered taking instead of Garnett were Texas's LaSalle Thompson, who would've helped fill a void at center, and Clark Kellogg, who was less of a fit because he played Aguirre's position.

STARTING TO LOOK LIKE A PLAYOFF TEAM ...

A 4-1 start in 1982-83 showed that the Mavericks were legit. Then came a 12-3 spurt in January and February. Dallas was a game over .500 at the All-Star break and still there with 11 games remaining in the season.

Then came the big fade. The Mavericks lost seven straight, won two, then lost the final two to finish at 38-44.

Owner Donald Carter's opening-night vow was right. They were contenders by their third season. Had the NBA expanded the playoffs to eight teams that season, instead of the next, Dallas would've had the eighth seed.

... WHICH MEANS NO LONGER RESEMBLING AN EXPANSION TEAM

Two of the final, favorite links to the original team were gone by Christmas 1982. Tom LaGarde left first, asking to be waived so that he could play in Italy.

"I've been drafted, traded, expanded and now waived. I guess you could say I'm a complete player," said LaGarde, whom fans voted their Favorite Maverick the inaugural season. "What makes me feel best about all of this is that it was my decision. For once, someone else wasn't deciding my future."

Scott Lloyd was waived in December, 1982, to make room for second-round pick Corny Thompson to come off the injured list. It was fitting that a guy known as "Corny" replaced Lloyd.

Among Lloyd's endearing moments was his victory in a pizza-eating contest, downing an entire large cheese pie in five minutes. On the court, he was the first Maverick with 10 assists; the strange part is that he was a 6-foot-10 center and it was the only time in his 372-game, six-year career that he had that many. During another game, he tied an NBA record with six fouls in one quarter.

"I enjoyed coaching him as much as any player I ever had," Motta said. "These things are going to happen on an expansion team. It was a talent decision. It hurt me very much."

"BEAT L.A.!" THEN "BEAT L.A.!" AGAIN

After winning the franchise opener, the next truly exciting victory came on November 17, 1982, against the Lakers at Reunion Arena. Although Dallas won in March in Los Angeles, doing it at home was better. And the way the Mavericks did it showed fans how much their hoots and hollers can help.

The Mavs were down by 16 in the third quarter, lulling the crowd to sleep. Then came the comeback—and the crowd. A loud roar went up when Aguirre made a three-pointer with 17 seconds left to get Dallas within two. Aguirre capped the rally by making another three-pointer, this one a bank shot off an inbounds pass with less than a second left and Jamaal Wilkes's hand in his face. Magic Johnson called it "miraculous."

"I just had to let it go," Aguirre said. "I didn't have time to dribble. I turned, shot and hoped it went in."

Carter was out of town, but his wife, Linda, had a phone by her and kept him posted. She treated the victory like a holiday, giving their kids the next day off from school.

Dallas beat the Lakers at Reunion again on February 2, 1983. The Mavericks came back from 14 down to win by two when Vincent tapped in a missed shot by Brad Davis just before the buzzer.

"People don't realize how much practice it takes to be able to shoot the ball so it comes off the rim into Jay's hands," Davis deadpanned.

Pat Cummings, a smallish center Dallas acquired from Milwaukee for a second-round pick, played a big role in both victories. He had 22 points and 17 rebounds in November, then 25 and 14 in February.

Kareem Abdul-Jabbar also had a big game in February, making 14 of 16 shots for 34 points the day after his home and most of his possessions were destroyed by fire. The team gave Abdul-Jabbar permission to stay away, but he took a late-night flight to Dallas. Reunion fans showed their appreciation by giving him a standing ovation.

AWESOME AGUIRRE

There was no sophomore slump for Mark Aguirre. It was more like he picked up where he left off from the pre-injury days of his rookie season. He was especially dominant during Dallas's 12-3 spurt during the 1982-83 season, breaking his own scoring record twice and recording the first triple-double in team history.

In the first game of the hot streak, he made a long three-pointer to tie the Clippers, then won it with an off-balance 20-footer.

The triple-double—30 points, 11 rebounds and 16 assists—came against Denver, and he had 13 assists in the first half. Two nights later, Aguirre had 32 points and 10 rebounds in a two-point loss to Utah.

With 43 points against Indiana, he beat his previous best by one. He upped it by one again with 44 points against Portland, a team Dallas had never beaten. He had 28 in the first-ever win over Phoenix. He had 32 points against Golden State, giving Motta his 600th career win.

In the last game of a five-game winning streak, Aguirre had 35 points, 11 rebounds against Kansas City.

Nonetheless, there were problems between the star player and his demanding coach. Motta even admitted he was prodding Aguirre so hard that he had "said things to him that I wouldn't say to my dog."

SUPPLEMENT SCARE

Before there was andro and ephedra, there was bee pollen.

Pat Cummings took bee pollen as a supplement a couple times with no problem. The third time, he broke out in hives, could barely breathe or swallow, and started turning red. He had to be hospitalized. Trainer Doug Atkinson said that without medication, Cummings could've died.

The stat line for him in the box score on February 16, 1983, read: DNP-Bee Pollen Reaction.

Cummings never tried the stuff again.

"It doesn't take a complicated mind to figure that out," he said.

Pollen-free, he became the first Maverick to grab 20 rebounds two weeks later.

4

Moody Madness

1983 DRAFT: THE CLEVELAND HAUL BEGINS

Dallas drafted two future All-Stars in 1983. Unfortunately, only Derek Harper made it as a Maverick. Dale Ellis was the other. He was taken ninth after the guy they really wanted, Antoine Carr, went eighth. Ellis's problem was that Mark Aguirre and Rolando Blackman already had established themselves as the main scoring threats and there was only one ball to go around.

Although Ellis set an NBA record with eight straight three-pointers his rookie season—when shots behind the arc were still pretty rare—he started only seven games in three seasons. He was traded to Seattle in July 1986 for Al Wood in one of the more forgettable deals in team history. Ellis was the league's Most Improved Player his first season as a Sonic and became an All-Star in 1989. He finished the '97-98 season with the most three-pointers in league history and retired with 19,002 points, the most of any player drafted by Dallas.

Harper was the 11th pick, taken with the first pick received from Cleveland (although it originally belonged to Atlanta). Harper spent two seasons as the understudy to Brad Davis, then was the Mavericks' top point guard well into the 1990s. He still holds the team records for assists, steals and three-pointers.

MAVS ARE "HAVES"

In 1983-84, the Mavericks were no longer up-and-comers. They arrived.

Dallas started 13-4, won its first 11 home games, and had an eight-game winning streak, the longest yet. The Mavs finished with 43 wins, their first winning season and first playoff berth. Mark Aguirre became the team's first All-Star and finished as the league's second leading scorer at 29.5 points per game.

In the postseason, Dallas won its first game and the first series thanks to the remarkable game known as "Moody Madness." Even now, that game symbolizes everything that was great about the Mavericks' rise to prominence.

"Moody Madness has been our measuring point," owner Donald Carter said in 1990. "It has been the benchmark to measure excitement and success, not of winning a championship, but the success of winning people's hearts."

Sports Illustrated began singing the team's praises in December. A writer working on a story about Magic Johnson saw Aguirre score 42 points as the Mavs routed the Lakers. It was Dallas's seventh straight win. The writer was so impressed that he called his editors and had his assignment changed. A four-page article was headlined, "The Mavs Have Joined the Haves."

Another sign of respect was when Frank Sinatra's manager requested a Mavericks jacket for Sinatra to wear during a concert at Reunion Arena. For some performers, such a gesture would be pandering to the crowd.

Not true for Sinatra.

Ol' Blue Eyes wasn't the only one who packed the house. The Mavericks had 11 sellouts and drew at least 10,000 people for 40 of 41 home games. The average attendance was 14,223—nearly double the first season.

ALL-STAR AGUIRRE

Aguirre was Player of the Week in November 1983 and Player of the Month the following January. He became the team's first All-Star in February and set the club scoring record for the fourth time in March.

"Mark is a star," Motta said. "I've never coached a star before. Not a real star. He's come a long way."

Aguirre led the team in scoring for 18 straight games and 24 of 25. During that stretch he had games of 42 points, 41, and two in a row with 40. He later had 46 against Denver. Another impressive performance was when he scored 38 on 16-of-25 shooting and had 10 assists in a 123-106 win at San Diego. It was the 100th victory in club history.

"I don't know of many guys who score that many points ... and still get 10 assists," Motta said.

Aguirre scored 2,330 points that season, still by far the most in team history. The next closest is 2,056, Aguirre's total in 1986-87. Dallas didn't have another player top 2,000 points until Dirk Nowitzki put up 2,011 in 2002-03.

RO GROWS

With Jay Vincent hurt, Rolando Blackman became the scorer teams had to fear when they double-teamed Aguirre. Blackman averaged 22.4 points in 1983-84. Among guards, only George Gervin scored more.

Aguirre and Blackman were quite a dynamic duo. Their combined average of 51.9 points was second only to the 55.8 from Denver's Kiki Vandeweghe and Alex English. There were many times when Aguirre and Blackman heated up the same night. The best example was March 24—against Vandeweghe, English and the Nuggets. While Aguirre was scoring a team-record 46, Blackman added 38. That came two weeks after Blackman set his career high with 43 against Golden State.

MOTTA "WHIPS IT"

During a game in Las Vegas, Dick Motta gambled that the referees had a sense of humor. The Mavericks were playing the Jazz in one of their home-away-from-home games. Dallas won 123-115, but the memorable part came during a timeout.

The San Diego Chicken was there to liven up the crowd, and one of his stunts involved beating up a dummy dressed as a referee to the tune of Devo's "Whip It." Motta stole the show by strolling onto the court and kicking the fake official.

"I've wanted to do that before," Motta said, presumably meaning during the routine and not with a real ref. "I wanted to do it at home last year, but we were eight down in the fourth quarter against Boston, and I didn't think we were going to win. It seemed more appropriate tonight."

The crowd loved it, and so did the Chicken. He went to the Dallas bench and kissed Motta's feet.

The officials didn't react, at least not that night. They made up for it, though, as Motta had an NBA-high 25 technical fouls that season.

MOODY MADNESS

Back when Reunion Arena officials set the spring 1984 schedule, they didn't think twice about having a WCT event on April 26. But doing so forced the Mavericks to play the fifth and deciding game of their first-ever playoff series in the scaled-down confines of Moody Coliseum on the SMU campus, setting the stage for one of the most amazing, bizarre and defining moments in team history.

First, the background. Dallas finished the regular season with one more win than Seattle, which was the difference between the fourth and fifth seeds. At fourth, the Mavericks had the home-court advantage. They needed all the help they could get because they were 1-4 against the SuperSonics that season, their worst record against any team.

Dick Motta often got stomping mad, especially at officials.
(NBAE/Getty Images)

The Sonics had a huge edge in playoff experience, featuring three players from their 1979 championship team—including stars Jack Sikma and Gus Williams. Dallas's entire playoff experience came from Pat Cummings and Roger Phegley.

Williams scored a playoff-record 23 points in the first quarter of the opener as Seattle went up by 16. The Mavericks hung in there, though, and a jumper by Blackman with 11 seconds left put Dallas ahead by one. Sikma then missed a layup, and Blackman added a free throw for an 88-86 victory in the franchise's first-ever playoff game.

Seattle led by 17 in the first half of Game 2, but the game again came down to the last minute. This time, Williams hit a three-pointer at the buzzer to tie the series at a game each.

Game 3 was played at the Seattle Coliseum instead of the Kingdome because—are you sitting down?—the Seahawks had the stadium reserved to show their highlight film to season ticket holders. They did reach the AFC championship game for the first and still only time, but still ...

The Sonics won Game 3 by 10, then returned to the Kingdome for Game 4. This time, the Mavericks coasted to an 11-point victory.

Now the scene was set for the deciding game. Game 5 at Moody Coliseum was a packed house as 9,007 fans—exactly 8,000 fewer than Reunion holds—showed up to support the home team. The college court had no three-point lines, so equipment manager Keith Grant spent 8 hours meticulously taping them down the day before.

With 48 seconds left in the game, Cummings made two free throws to get Dallas within four. Seattle blundered by not getting the ball across halfcourt in time—twice. Blackman missed a layup the first time, but dunked the second to narrow Seattle's lead to two points.

Then Aguirre commited a foul before the clock even started. That gave the Sonics a free throw and possession of the ball, a potentially game-ending combination. Incredibly, no damage was done. Al Wood missed the foul shot, and Steve Hawes—playing because Sikma fouled out—couldn't get off the inbounds pass, even though Seattle had called time to set up a play.

The Mavs went back to Blackman. His jumper from the top of the key hit the front of the rim, then the backboard, and dropped in for a tie with 15 seconds remaining.

Seattle didn't get the final shot it wanted. Fred Brown put up a 22-footer that missed. Danny Vranes tipped it back onto the rim, but it still didn't go down.

In overtime, the Mavericks were up 105-102 when Jay Vincent went to the foul line with just five seconds left. He had made 31 straight free throws. But he missed the first. And the second.

Then Seattle's Tom Chambers tipped in a shot to bring Seattle within one point with one tick left on the clock.

Timeout, Dallas.

Vincent was ready to inbound the ball at halfcourt with Chambers defending him. Vincent tried bouncing the ball off of Chambers, but Chambers caught the pass and flung a 50-footer that didn't even come close to going in.

Referee Mike Mathis signaled that the game was over, and the Mavericks ran to the locker room in delight—even though the clock still showed 0:01 remaining. For 14 minutes, Mathis confered with the rest of the officiating crew—Jake O'Donnell and Tommy Nunez—about what to do. Seattle players and coaches pled their case while fans alternately chanted, "We want L.A." and "Go home Seattle."

O'Donnell ruled that Mathis blew his whistle inadvertently. The Sonics got the ball back because Chambers had stolen it. Meanwhile, some Mavericks in the locker room already had their shoes off. Others were headed to the showers when they were called back to the court.

Hawes tried lobbing the ball to Chambers, but Aguirre and Kurt Nimphius knocked it away. *Finally*, it was game, set and match.

*Dick Motta and Pat Cummings start celebrating the Game 5 win over
Seattle a little too soon. Notice the :01 left on the clock.
(NBAE/Getty Images)*

Oops, wrong sport. That's what was happening at Reunion.

At Moody, the buzzer settled the game and the series—a series, by the way, in which the cumulative score was Dallas 486, Seattle 485, with the last four games played in four different buildings.

"Man," Motta said, "what a wild finish."

HARPER DRIBBLES OUT THE CLOCK

A day and a half later, the Mavericks were in Los Angeles facing a team that had been off for six days. Fresh legs at home versus tired ones on the road is a dangerous combination. The result: Los Angeles led by 20 in the first quarter and ended up winning by 43.

The Mavericks resembled a playoff team in Game 2, but they still lost by 16.

Returning to Reunion for Game 3 invigorated the Mavs. They went ahead late in the first quarter and never let go. Blackman scored 31, Ellis made eight of 10 off the bench, and Cummings grabbed twice as many rebounds as Kareem Abdul-Jabbar in a 10-point victory.

A lot was riding on Game 4. Either Dallas would tie the series or Los Angeles would move to within a win of the conference finals. Adding to the drama was the fact that this was the first time CBS showed a game from Reunion Arena. Viewers got quite a treat. The Mavericks rallied from 11 down to tie it at 98 on a layup by Harper. The Lakers went back up by five; then Dallas scored six straight. Two free throws from Michael Cooper put the Lakers back on top.

With 54 seconds left, Aguirre dove for a rebound and hurt his hip, forcing him out of the game. Dallas tied it at 108 on a layup by Cummings, who was also fouled on the play. He stepped to the line after hitting14 of 14 free throws in the playoffs. One more would put the Mavs ahead.

He missed.

On the Lakers' next possession, Abdul-Jabbar missed his trademark skyhook. Blackman grabbed the rebound and fired a pass to Ellis, who threw it to Harper with six seconds left. Harper, though, thought Dallas was ahead and didn't even look at the basket. He just kept dribbling until time ran out.

Everyone who saw it remembers helplessly screaming at Harper to do something—*anything!*—while he contentedly bounced the ball. Teammates and coaches were bewildered. Harper was just as confused by their reaction until he realized what he'd done.

Yet Harper didn't sulk. He opened overtime with a long jumper, then stole the ball from Cooper, leading to two free throws by Vincent and a four-point lead. Then Vincent fouled out, and the Lakers wound up winning 122-115.

Over the years, fuzzy memories leave many people thinking Harper dribbled away a victory. But all he did was force overtime, which would've happened anyway if he'd missed a shot or passed to someone else who missed. The game was not lost because of him, although his blunder cost Dallas a chance to win.

Afterward, the 22-year-old rookie answered every question from every reporter, including the critical ones. The way he handled it earned lasting praise and admiration.

Game 5 didn't turn out any better. Aguirre didn't start and scored only nine points in 14 minutes. The Mavericks lost 115-99, ending their best season—thus far.

REUNION ROWDIES: BIRTH OF A NICKNAME

The game known for Harper's gaffe also was the day the phrase "Reunion Rowdies" was born. Jan Hubbard, who had covered the team since its inception, used the phrase in a story in that day's *Dallas Morning News.*

"It was intended as nothing more than a casual reference," he wrote in the team's 20th anniversary yearbook. "But on Sunday afternoon, I looked up into the upper deck and two guys were carrying around a large sign that said, 'Reunion Rowdies.'

"While I have to admit that it is always fun to find that the name is still used, I wish I would have gone to the upper deck to find out who made the sign, because whoever it was gave the name its permanence."

THE "MODEL" FRANCHISE

In four seasons, the Mavericks had become a championship contender and proved that Dallas wasn't just a football city.

The team also was a raging success financially. When they sent the league a check for $1,320,000 on September 1, 1985, to pay off the balance on the original franchise fee, the funds came strictly from profit. The second-to-last payment did, too.

"I think they've certainly surpassed anybody's expectations for being a model for creating a new sports franchise," NBA executive vice president Russ Granik told *The Dallas Morning News.* "There's no question that they did it right, and I don't think you can sit back and say that it was luck in any way."

5

A Bump in the Road

1984 DRAFT

With the fourth and 15th picks in the 1984 draft, the Mavericks took Sam Perkins and Terence Stansbury. But they could've had Charles Barkley and John Stockton. Barkley went fifth to Philadelphia. Stockton went 16th to Utah.

Just like in 1982, Dallas went into the draft with the fourth pick when there were three clear-cut favorites: Akeem (no "H" back then) Olajuwon, Sam Bowie and Michael Jordan. (While history puts Jordan first, this was the order they were drafted.) The Mavericks got the fourth pick from the Cavaliers. Had Cleveland lost twice more the previous season, Dallas would've had the third pick and would've taken Jordan; Sund loved him.

Getting Perkins, Jordan's teammate at North Carolina, wasn't like settling for Bill Garnett. Perkins had a successful career in Dallas, so there's not much second-guessing.

But Stansbury? A contract squabble made him late to training camp, and two weeks later he and Garnett were traded. Stansbury lasted only three seasons in the NBA. If he's remembered at all, it's for reaching the semifinals of the All-Star dunk contest all three of his seasons, including 1986 in Dallas.

SAM'S START

Sam Perkins started his career playing out of position at center. As if that wasn't tough enough, in his first eight games he faced Houston's Twin Towers of Ralph Sampson and Olajuwon (twice), Kareem Abdul-Jabbar and Moses Malone.

Perkins flourished once he went back to forward. He wound up on the All-Rookie first team.

"He's the best defensive big forward I've ever coached," Motta said that season. "Once he started working at forward, you could see him pick up the subtle aspects of my offense."

There's a funny story about Perkins's arrival in Dallas. After a holdout, he came straight from Los Angeles, where he'd helped Team USA win a gold medal at the '84 Olympics. He was wearing his prize when he went out to dinner with media services director Kevin Sullivan and broadcaster Allen Stone, but Perkins forgot his medal in Stone's car.

Perkins got the medal back the next day and wore it to his introductory news conference. Then Stone drove him to the team doctor's office for a physical, and again Perkins left the medal under the front seat. This time, Stone and Sullivan had some fun, letting colleagues pose for pictures with it.

"Most people can only dream of winning a gold medal," Stone said. "Sam won one and couldn't seem to hold onto it."

A SLIPPERY STORY

Whoever put preservatives on the Reunion Arena court to protect it during the off season apparently got a little carried away. The surface came out so slick that the start of a preseason game against the Philadelphia 76ers was delayed while cleanup crews tried making it safe. Less than two minutes into the game, Philadelphia's Maurice Cheeks went down, and the game was stopped. A 26-person crew spent the next 37 minutes scrubbing the floor with mops, brooms and cleanser.

When play resumed, Rolando Blackman went down hard on his left hip while backpedaling on defense. That was it. The game was called off after eight minutes, 41 seconds.

"It was not a difficult decision," Sonju said.

One reason not obvious to all: Three hours earlier, Blackman had signed a 10-year contract extension.

The Mavericks faced another slippery floor on March 11, 1999, causing the start of a game against the Phoenix Suns to be delayed 78 minutes. Officiating crew chief Bennett Salvatore said the game had been in danger of not being played. Mavericks coach Don Nelson gave players the option of sitting it out, and oft-injured guard Robert Pack was the only one who accepted.

I'LL SHOW YOU WHAT AN ALL-STAR LOOKS LIKE!

On January 28, 1985, Mark Aguirre wasn't wondering whether he'd be invited back for a second All-Star game. His only question was whether Blackman would be joining him.

Ro made it. But Mark didn't. And for the next month, Aguirre took it out on every team Dallas played.

Aguirre started by setting the club scoring record for the fifth time, pouring in 49 points in a 111-109 victory over the 76ers.

"He had that look in his eye," Julius Erving said.

"It was like he was trying to let the Western coaches know they had a made a mistake," Philadelphia coach Billy Cunningham said.

Aguirre had 40 against Detroit, 45 against Washington and 46 against Denver.

It wasn't production that kept him off the squad. It was attitude. On December 18, Motta pulled Aguirre from a 110-96 loss against Milwaukee for not hustling, prompting a face-to-face confrontation in the locker room. Motta accused Aguirre of quitting on his teammates and called him a "coward." Aguirre shot back that Motta should trade him. Motta said he'd rather let Aguirre rot on the bench than "make a fool out of me."

BEFORE CHALUPAS,
THERE WERE BIG-TOPPER PIZZAS

Dale Ellis became the Pizza Man in 1984-85.

In a promotion that long preceded free chalupas from Taco Bell, Pizza Hut offered fans a free "Big Topper" pizza if the Mavs scored 125 and won. It happened four times, and Ellis scored the pizza points every time.

"I was just in the right place at the right time," said Ellis, who received a red and white jacket that said "Pizza Man."

WEIRD SEASON ENDS WITH BITTER EXIT

The Mavericks were so healthy in 1984-85 that they lost only six player-games to injury, believed to be the fewest in league history. They played before sellout crowds almost every home game. And they won almost as many road games as they lost, going 20-21.

Still, things never quite worked out as well as expected.

Dallas won seven fewer games at home than the previous season. The Mavs never won more than four straight, yet never lost more than three. They overcame a 19-point deficit and blew a 23-point lead.

They went into the playoffs with a streak to uphold: The franchise had progressed by a playoff round per season. To keep it up, the Mavericks had to get to the conference finals. But they didn't make it out of the first round.

Dallas won Game 1 against Portland in double overtime, then dropped the next two. The Blazers closed it out in Game 4 when Audie "The Atomic Dog" Norris hit a running hook with 22 seconds left, then a 10-foot jumper with one second to go in a 115-113 victory.

Rolando Blackman had 43 and 41 points the first two games and averaged 32.8 for the series. Clyde Drexler was so impressed that when asked how to stop Blackman, he said, "Get a gun and shoot him."

6

All-Star Success

'85 DRAFT: A FOREIGN CONCEPT; WHAT WASN'T DELIVERED

On June 18, 1985, the day before Dirk Nowitzki turned seven and a few months before Steve Nash started sixth grade, the Mavericks spent three first-round draft picks on two German-born players (Detlef Schrempf and Uwe Blab) and a Canadian (Bill Wennington).

All three were supposed to answer problems. None did.

While Schrempf eventually became an All-Star and the Sixth Man of the Year and Wennington collected a drawer full of championship rings, their glory came after leaving Dallas. Rather than question how the Mavericks handled them, a better discussion is why they were even drafted.

Dallas went into the draft desperate for a center, but the best four were gone when the Mavs picked at No. 8. Looking for depth, they took Schrempf instead of Karl Malone because the German was so versatile. He could play small forward, forward or even center. Malone badly wanted to be a Maverick and even had a Dallas-based agent. The Mavericks did make a pitch for him, offering Jay Vincent to Washington for the 12th pick. The Bullets, though, preferred to draft Kenny Green. That allowed Malone to slide all the way to the 13th pick.

While missing on Malone is the big story now, the draft was popular with fans at the time because of the addition of the two centers. Fans even chanted Blab's name before he was announced.

SEEKING THE ELUSIVE MAN IN THE MIDDLE

Dallas had been seeking an elite center since day one. The leadership committee figured they'd eventually draft one, especially after getting all the picks from Cleveland. By 1985, it still hadn't happened. Management was so desperate that the Mavericks spent the 16th pick on Wennington and 17th on Blab.

"We have a nice stable of quality perimeter players," Motta said. "If one of the two hit, we're going to be a very nice basketball team."

The center quandary was all Mavericks fans were talking about—partly because it's all the team was talking about. It was such a hot topic that Larry King mentioned it in his *USA Today* column, throwing out a line about the Mavericks being title contenders—if only they had a center.

ANOTHER DREAM TEAM
OR WHAT COULD HAVE BEEN?

This probably isn't fair to the Mavericks' draft gurus. And it's certainly a harsh tease for longtime fans. Still, it's amazing to consider the roster Dallas could've built between the '82, '83, '84 and '85 drafts and some existing players:

At point guard the team could have drafted John Stockton or Brad Davis and of course did draft Derek Harper. As for shooting guards, the team made the right call in taking Rolando Blackman, but passed on Joe Dumars. In addition to Mark Aguirre, the Mavs also had a shot at Clyde Drexler, who was taken 14th in the 1983 draft after Dallas took Dale Ellis ninth and Derek Harper 11th.

As for power forwards, the Mavericks missed two great ones in Karl Malone and Charles Barkley, despite nabbing Jay Vincent. At center, the team passed on LaSalle Thompson and even Manute Bol (what the heck; it wouldn't matter on a roster like this, and the 7-foot-7 novelty was available when Dallas took Blab and Wennington, eventually going 31st to Washington).

BIG JAMES

The Mavericks finally found their big man on November 25, 1985, when they sent Kurt Nimphius to the Los Angeles Clippers for James Donaldson.

"He is better than anyone we have as a true center, and he is better than whom we had to give up," Motta said. "We are not bringing him here to be a big scorer. We are bringing him here because of his size."

At 7-foot-2, 278 pounds, Donaldson certainly had the size. But he'd only been a fourth-round pick, had spent a year in Italy and had five so-so seasons with the Sonics and Clippers.

Donaldson received a rousing ovation at his first home game and responded with nine points and 11 rebounds in 26 minutes. The next night, Motta not-so-subtly jabbed at everyone who'd been gnashing their teeth over the center woes by using a lineup of Donaldson, Blab, Wennington, 6-foot-10 Schrempf and Harper for the final 4:17 of a lopsided win over Sacramento.

"Coach was thinking of subbing me in at guard," said 6-foot-10 Sam Perkins. "I would have liked it. I would have run the plays for the forwards."

Donaldson became a starter by his sixth game and finished the season with 9.6 rebounds per game, the best yet in club history. Donaldson, who eventually became an All-Star, also stopped a merry-go-round of centers starting the season opener. When he handled the tipoff in 1987, he became the seventh different starter in the franchise's first seven seasons, following Tom LaGarde, Scott

Lloyd, Kurt Nimphius, Pat Cummings, Sam Perkins and Wallace Bryant. Donaldson held the job for the next five openers.

STUCK IN NEUTRAL

The 1985-86 season was the first time the Mavericks didn't win more games than the previous season. But at least they didn't go backwards. In going 44-38—again—there were plenty of memorable moments.

Sam Perkins posted 31 points, 20 rebounds and seven assists in a 123-120 loss to Houston. It's still the only 30-20 game in team history.

On January 22, Dallas was 19-19 when coach Dick Motta shifted point guards, starting Derek Harper. That ended Brad Davis's streak of 120 straight starts (and 238 of 239).

"It's not Brad's fault we aren't playing to our potential," Motta said.

The Mavs lost that game to fall below .500, but went 25-18 the rest of the season.

The Chicago Bulls came to Reunion and received a huge performance from a player not named Michael Jordan. Old nemesis George Gervin scored 35 first-half points and finished with 45 for the game.

"I've never seen a better half by anybody," Harper said.

Gervin was wearing shoes from his Spurs days that a friend had brought to him at Reunion Arena.

PROBLEMS WITH AGUIRRE

By December 1985, Aguirre seemed to have forgotten the image of the stake on Donald Carter's ranch, the sight the owner hoped would scare him straight.

In a 20-point loss at Boston on December 18, Motta pulled Aguirre for not hustling. Motta then told Aguirre to improve in

Mark Aguirre and Dick Motta often pointed in different directions.
(NBAE/Getty Images)

four areas: getting back on defense, blocking out for rebounds, avoiding reach-in fouls in the open court and controlling his emotions in front of officials. He'd get one freebie, but a second violation would land him on the bench. Aguirre said he understood.

The next night in Atlanta, Aguirre broke the first rule after a missed shot and was taken out of the game. He returned and did it again. That second time, Aguirre collided with Dominique Wilkins. Then, instead of running back on defense, he stopped to help Wilkins get up. Aguirre was benched again—for breaking the rule, not for helping the opposition. Motta told Aguirre to go back in during the second half. Aguirre refused. The next day, he was suspended without pay for "insubordination and conduct detrimental to the team." It cost him more than $15,000 and likely kept him out of the All-Star Game—in Dallas. Aguirre ended up apologizing and returned to the team for a practice on Christmas Eve.

When Aguirre was focused, he remained a tremendous force. He had a triple-double in November and in March scored 40 and 42 points in consecutive games.

THE DOCTOR'S FINAL HOUSE CALL(S)

Dr. J's last shot in Reunion Arena was a 50-foot game-winning swish.

On February 28, 1986, a Philadelphia-Dallas game was tied at 120 with two seconds left. Maurice Cheeks handed the ball to an unguarded Erving at midcourt, and he nailed it.

"I never have hit one exactly like that," said Erving, who was the star of the first game the Mavericks played in Reunion Arena, scoring 22 points in Philadelphia's 113-108 victory over Dallas in a September 1980 exhibition game.

A year later, a finger injury kept Erving from playing in Dallas during his farewell season. He came anyway, and the Mavericks honored him by donating more than $40,000 to the Julius Erving Lupus Research Fund. He also was given a sculpture that he said was going into his trophy case.

"I'll look at it when—and it's eventually going to happen—the Mavericks win their first NBA title," Erving told a delighted crowd.

DALLAS AND REUNION: THE REAL ALL-STARS

The NBA's best of the present and the past arrived in Dallas for a celebration on February 8-9, 1986, and everyone went home happy.

Tiny Spud Webb, who grew up in the area, soared to stardom as the stunning winner of the dunk contest. Larry Bird backed up his boasting and won the inaugural three-point contest. "Pistol" Pete Maravich proved that he was still firing even in retirement as the leading scorer in the Legends game. And in the All-Star Game, Rolando Blackman had 12 points and eight assists, but Isiah Thomas led the East to a 139-132 victory.

"How are we going to top this?" NBA commissioner David Stern asked. "On a scale of 10, I'd give Dallas an 11 for this entire weekend."

Some writers were so impressed that they floated the idea of Reunion being the permanent site for the event.

Bird went into the three-point contest telling everyone he was going to win. He backed it up by making 11 straight shots to beat Milwaukee's Craig Hodges in the finals, winning $10,000 and a trip to Hawaii.

"I just wanted to know who was going to come in second," he said.

Bird's victory made sense. But Webb's?

At 5-foot-7, wearing size seven shoes that seemed spring-loaded, the NBA's smallest player beat "The Human Highlight Film," defending dunk champion Dominique Wilkins.

Three of Webb's dunks got perfect scores—two for 360-degree spins and another for bouncing the ball over the rim, catching it with one hand as it came off the backboard and slamming it down in the same motion.

"I couldn't have done what he did," raved Michael Jordan, who could only watch because of a foot injury.

In the Legends game, Maravich's hot shooting wasn't enough for the East as 48-year-old Oscar Robertson had eight points, seven assists and four rebounds to guide the West to the victory.

A party at the Dallas Convention Center headlined by Willie Nelson capped the fun on Saturday. The main event was on Sunday.

Blackman was cheered so loudly and for so long that it gave him "too many goose bumps to count." But Thomas scored 30 points on 11-of-19 shooting to earn MVP honors.

LONG-DISTANCE DEDICATION

On January 28, 1985, Philadelphia's Leon Wood was working on—and showing off—his incredible three-point range hours before a game in Reunion Arena. His performance drew a small crowd of fans. Mavs marketing director Greg Jamison stopped to watch, too, and was as captivated by the audience's response as he was by Wood's jumpers.

"Every time he hit a shot, the people would go crazy," said Jamison, now the president and chief executive officer of the group that owns the NHL's San Jose Sharks. "He started backing up and was barely inbounds. I think he was three, four, five feet behind the line and was still making them. Then he drains his last shot and trots off to a standing ovation."

Still wowed by the scene days later, Jamison described it during a staff meeting and suggested that a three-point shooting contest be held during the 1986 All-Star weekend, which the team was helping plan. The idea was well received, so the Mavericks passed it along to the league office. There's some question about whether the NBA already was working on a similar concept, which is why Jamison has never received full credit as the event's founder. But everyone in the Mavericks organization knows they heard it from him first.

"Whoever took the idea and enhanced it has done a great job with it," Jamison said. "It's a true skill contest. Larry Bird helped substantiate that when he won it."

"DALLAS 116, BOSTON 115 ... FINALLY"

That was the title of a 22-minute video the Mavericks sold commemorating "the greatest regular-season win in club history."

On March 10, 1986, a Boston team on its way to winning the NBA title came into Reunion Arena with an all-time record of 11-0 against Dallas. Aguirre was out with the flu, Harper was playing on a sprained ankle, and Jay Vincent was battling flu symptoms.

After trailing by 13 with 5:37 left, Dallas went ahead by one on two free throws by Brad Davis with 56 seconds left. Dale Ellis, who had been one of seven, hit a three-pointer to stretch the lead to four. Bird hit a three-pointer between two defenders with nine seconds left to get Boston within one, but Davis upped the lead with two more free throws. Bird followed with a layup, giving him 50 points—matching the most by a Dallas opponent— but it left the Celtics down by a point when time ran out.

After 474 games, the Mavericks finally had beaten all 22 teams.

"It was going to happen eventually," Motta said, "whether I'm the coach here or Rip Van Winkle."

The Celtics thought so little of their performance that Walton later told Bird he had "the worst game ever in the history of the NBA by someone who scored 50 points." It's the kind of comment that helped Walton become a popular broadcaster—a second career, by the way, that was boosted by working Mavericks games in the early 1990s.

HARPER'S REDEMPTION

With Adrian Dantley, the league's leading scorer, out with an injury, the Mavericks beat Utah in four games in the first round of the 1985-86 playoffs.

Dallas won the first two at home and nearly had a sweep until rookie Karl Malone hit a turnaround jumper to put Utah up 100-98 with 50 seconds left in Game 3. Blackman missed a chance to tie it in the closing seconds.

The Mavs closed out the series in the next game as Davis set an NBA playoff record by going five for five on three-pointers. Most importantly, it set up another semifinal showdown with the Lakers.

Los Angeles won the first two games at home, and Dallas took the next two at Reunion. Game 3 was special because Derek Harper led the way to victory. In the first playoff game against

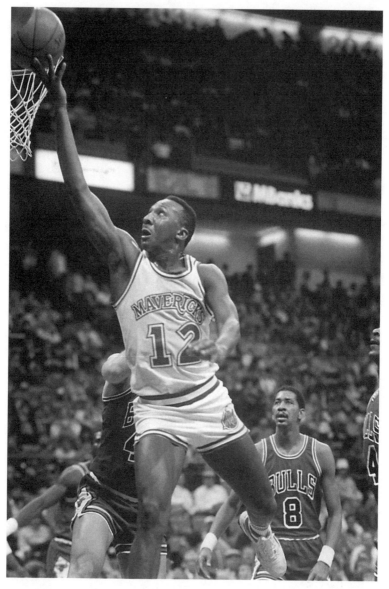

Derek Harper was a stand-up guy for the way he handled his dribble-out-the-clock gaffe in the 1983 playoffs. In the 1985 playoffs, he got his sweet revenge. (NBAE/Getty Images)

the Lakers at Reunion since he infamously dribbled out the clock, Harper redeemed himself by remaining cool under pressure in the final minute. He hit a game-tying three-pointer with 46 seconds left, then caught an errant pass from James Worthy and nailed a three-pointer with three seconds left for a 110-108 win.

"I hope this puts two years ago to rest," said Harper, who was 10 of 14 with 24 points in the game and averaged 16.5 points and 8.8 assists in the series.

Mark Aguirre nearly had a triple-double that game (27 points, nine rebounds and eight assists) and was fabulous again in Game 4, scoring 21 points in the first quarter and 39 total. The last two came on a turnaround jumper from the left baseline in the final seconds that gave the Mavericks a 120-118 win.

After the Lakers won Game 5 at the Forum, Dallas was hoping the home-team winning streak would continue in Game 6. It didn't. Aguirre, who scored 12 of his game-high 28 while the Mavericks whittled a 20-point deficit down to two, sprained an ankle in the third quarter. After taking himself out of the game, he hardly played in the fourth quarter as Los Angeles eliminated Dallas again.

7

The Wreck at the Hec

UNDOING A DONE DEAL

Both sides agreed it was done. In June 1986, Lakers owner Jerry Buss promised to send James Worthy to the Mavericks for Mark Aguirre and the seventh pick in the upcoming draft, which became Roy Tarpley. There was even talk of Mavs owner Donald Carter throwing in Tatu, the star of the Dallas Sidekicks, an indoor soccer league team that Carter owned. He would've been dealt to the Buss-owned Lazers in a seperate, but connected, trade.

Buss negotiated the swap on the recommendation of Aguirre's pal, Magic Johnson. Buss thought he could convince general manager Jerry West to go along because he thought West coveted Tarpley.

But West was so against the trade that he threatened to quit. So Buss called Carter back, tracking him down at a hospital where Carter was visiting his ill mother.

"I made a deal, I'll stick with it," Buss said. "I don't want to, but I will. It may cost me my GM."

Carter let Buss off the hook, mostly out of respect for West. Then Carter's mother died about two weeks later; Aguirre's mother died soon after, too. Sorrow bonded them, prompting Carter to declare that Aguirre couldn't be traded for two months because he needed stability in his life.

"I felt like Mark was close to a breaking point," Carter said. "I wasn't willing to take the chance of having it on my conscience."

The Mavericks honored the memory of Mary Crowley, Carter's mother, by wearing black bands with a green stripe for the first two months of the next season. Aguirre, whose mother also was named Mary, had her name stitched onto every pair of hightops he wore that season.

1986 DRAFT: CLEVELAND'S PAYBACK

Drafting Tarpley at No. 7 was an easy choice with all sorts of ramifications that will be detailed later. Here we'll examine what Dallas did with the first pick of the second round.

The Mavericks chose Mark Price, who would become a four-time All-Star. But they never planned on keeping him. Price was taken for Cleveland as part of a prearranged deal that gave Dallas the 35th pick. The Mavericks used it on Milt Wagner, who didn't make the team. (Milt is now known for his son, Dejuan Wagner, a young star for ... Cleveland.)

Considering all the great first-round picks that came from the Cavaliers—including Tarpley—it seems only fair that they at least got the better end of one deal with Dallas.

GETTING DEFENSIVE

Defense wasn't very popular in the 1980s. In 1985-86, the champion Celtics allowed 104.7 points per game—and that was third best in the league. Dallas was on the opposite end, allowing the third most points at 114.2. Good thing the Mavs scored 115.3.

So when Bob Weiss left to coach the Spurs, Dallas decided his replacement would specialize in defense. Motta wanted Jerry Sloan, a gritty player he'd coached for eight seasons in Chicago. But Sloan remained in Utah as an assistant to Frank Layden.

Dallas instead went with Richie Adubato, who'd helped the Knicks produce the league's stingiest defense in two of his four seasons there. He made his mark on opening day. Avenging the 1980 "Halloween Massacre," the Mavericks beat Utah 103-77 on October 31.

"We still have our beautiful people," Rolando Blackman said. "But we're definitely going to get down in the grass and start tumbling a bit more."

The Jazz had only 10 points in the first quarter, still tied for the fewest Dallas has ever allowed. They scored 30 by halftime and shot just .311 for the game.

"They manhandled us," grumbled the normally upbeat Layden.

Derek Harper ended up making the All-Defense second team, the first time a Maverick ever made that squad. The season also marked the beginning of a run of four straight years in which opponent scoring decreased.

A WILD RIDE

There's not really an easy way to get to the Hopi Indian Reservation in Kykotsmovi, Arizona. In October 1986, following an exhibition game against the Phoenix Suns, the Mavericks learned it's just as tough to get back.

Dallas's journey began on a 33-seat, twin-prop plane used by country singer Charlie Pride. The team flew into Winslow, Arizona—the town made famous by the Eagles song "Take It Easy"—then had a 70-mile bus ride to the Hopi Civic Center.

About 3,300 people crammed into the 2,500-seat arena, with another 3,000 turned away. Phoenix won 105-97.

"This was the first NBA game on an Indian reservation, and I got the first technical," coach Dick Motta said. "I had great apprehensions about coming here. But just to look at those kids' faces made it worth it. It was a tremendous experience."

Actually, the experience was only beginning.

The flight home started in a thunderstorm, with rain pelting the plane and lightning visible outside the windows. Then, high above New Mexico, a light came on telling pilots an engine was failing, forcing an emergency landing in Albuquerque and many knotted stomachs—except for Sam Perkins, who slept through it all.

Once safely on the ground, there was some confusion over whether there really was a problem or just a faulty light. The alternator was replaced anyway, and the team flew home on the same plane. To try instilling some much-needed peace of mind, the mechanic joined them.

"I sat back and prayed," Aguirre said.

ROY'S ROOKIE SEASON

While preseason isn't the best way to judge a player, it was still impressive seeing Tarpley hit double digits in points and rebounds in less than 25 minutes against Utah, Philadelphia and Boston, all playoff teams.

"He hit his first four jumpers on me," Larry Bird said. "That showed me something."

Tarpley began thinking the NBA was going to be easy. He soon learned that pure talent only carried him so far. Tarpley looked lost at times in his first five games, taking—and missing—bad shots and picking up silly fouls. He sat out four of the next five games and started to get the message coaches were sending him.

He began developing once he improved his work habits, conditioning and focus. That included dropping 15 pounds of fat he'd brought to training camp. Tarpley became a fixture after putting up 14 points and 13 rebounds against New York on January 21. He had a team-best 12 rebounds two games later, then 20 the next game. He averaged 7.1 rebounds in just 18.7 minutes. Projected over 48 minutes, that's 18.2 boards per game.

THAT'S WHAT I'M TALKING ABOUT!

Rolando Blackman stood at the free throw line of the Seattle Kingdome with no time left on the clock and the West All-Stars down by two. Isiah Thomas was doing his best to ruin Blackman's concentration. Magic Johnson was doing his best to restrain Thomas. Blackman did his best to focus on the rim, sinking the first shot.

"Confidence, baby, confidence!" Blackman screamed as he released the second shot.

Bingo. Overtime.

Blackman finished with 29 points in 22 minutes as the West beat the East 154-149 in the highest-scoring All-Star Game. He finished second in MVP voting to hometown star Tom Chambers, who scored 34 points.

STOOGES, EH? WELL, I OUGHTA ... SUSPEND YOU

Dick Motta didn't think the Houston Rockets were trying very hard, and he didn't hesitate to say so.

After seeing Akeem Olajuwon, Ralph Sampson and Rodney McCray on the bench in the fourth quarter of a tied game with Phoenix, Motta accused Houston of trying to lose, presumably to finagle a playoff seeding to avoid the Lakers as long as possible.

"The camera kept looking at the three stooges all together," Motta said. "They were happy. They were laughing ... Houston looks like they're messing around ... manipulating ... It was about the most blatant I've ever seen. It wasn't even cute."

It wasn't the first time the Rockets were accused of sandbagging. In fact, the way they played late in the '83-84 season led to the creation of the coin flip for the first pick, the forerunner to the lottery.

*With Magic taming Isiah, Rolando Blackman shows real
"confidence, baby, confidence" at the All-Star Game.
(NBAE/Getty Images)*

Houston coach Bill Fitch said Motta made "frivolous statements" and that "the commissioner or our owner will take him to task ... Dick Motta, who I've always thought was a smart man, did a dumb thing."

Motta replied that he was trying to uphold the integrity of the league, saying, "The whole American way is designed to win every game you can and do the very best you can all the time."

The NBA suspended Motta without pay for one game and fined the team $5,000 for failing to censor him.

EVERYTHING COMING TOGETHER

With a little more defense and a lot of Tarpley, the Mavericks had a memorable 1986-87 regular season. Motta won his 800th game, Aguirre scored his 10,000th career point and James Donaldson averaged 11.9 rebounds a game, fourth best in the league and still the team record. Tarpley made the All-Rookie team, while Aguirre and Blackman were All-Stars. Dallas also traded Dale Ellis and Jay Vincent, clearing playing time for Detlef Schrempf. On January 30, he started in place of an injured Blackman and produced the franchise's third triple-double (15-10-10), the first by someone other than Aguirre.

The Mavericks never lost more than two in a row and won a franchise-best 55 games. They won 20 road games, even though they returned to the blue uniforms shelved after the charter season.

Best of all, Dallas captured its first—and still only—Midwest Division title.

The Mavericks roared into the playoffs by winning 15 of the last 19. And the first-round foe was Seattle, a team they'd gone 5-0 against, winning by an average of 18.6 points.

Everything was looking up for the Mavericks when this banner was raised on April 23, 1987, prior to losing to No. 7 seed Seattle. (NBAE/Getty Images)

"THE WRECK AT THE HEC"

Before Game 1 of the Seattle series, the Mavericks raised a banner proclaiming them Midwest Division champions. Then they razed the SuperSonics.

Ten players scored in double figures as Dallas racked up 151 points, the most in team history and the fourth best in NBA playoff history. The Mavs led by as many as 38 and won by 22, even letting 12th man Dennis Nutt score the 150th point.

Considering how easily Dallas had handled Seattle in the regular season, too, the *Fort Worth Star-Telegram* was merely summing up the mood when it ran a headline the next day that read, "Is Mavericks-Sonics series really necessary?"

Then everything fell apart.

A tense, back-and-forth Game 2 was tied with four seconds left when former Maverick Dale Ellis tried passing the ball to center Clemon Johnson. Dallas had a foul to give, so Sam Perkins whacked Ellis's arms. Officials said Ellis was shooting and gave him two free throws. He hit both and Seattle won 112-110. Adding injury to insult, Donaldson was diagnosed with a stress reaction in his right leg that would require surgery after the playoffs.

The series returned to Seattle, but not to the Coliseum where the Sonics usually played. An agricultural convention was booked there, and the Kingdome, their backup site, was being used for baseball. So in a move eerily reminiscent of Moody Madness, the next two games were played at the 8,150-seat Hec Edmundson Pavilion on the University of Washington campus. Dallas cut a 22-point deficit to six in the final two minutes of Game 3, but lost by 10.

Facing elimination in Game 4, the Mavericks could do nothing about it. They trailed 11-2 and never recovered, losing 124-98 exactly one week after a lopsided Game 1 win had fans plotting routes for the championship parade.

With this "Wreck at the Hec," Dallas became the first No. 2 seed to lose to a No. 7 since the playoffs were expanded in 1984. It also was the first three-game losing skid of the season.

Still, no one was prepared for what happened next.

8

Goodbye Motta, Hello Conference Finals

MOTTA'S DEPARTURE

The franchise was practically in mourning. No one could believe the collapse. GM Norm Sonju went on TV and apologized to fans. He told everyone in the organization to lay low.

Of all the possible changes, a new coach wasn't among them. Owner Donald Carter had already laid out a lifetime contract for Dick Motta that was renewable at Motta's option. After the playoff wipeout, he shook Carter's hand and said he'd be back.

Then Motta's wanderlust kicked in. Just like he'd openly coveted the Dallas job while in Washington, he began talking about what he could do with the Knicks and Clippers. He also reportedly was interested in Phoenix.

Motta took three days to decline an interview request with the lowly Clippers, and he accepted the Knicks' invitation to visit New York. What angered Mavericks fans the most was Motta telling a New York reporter, "I can probably win 50 games in Dallas over the next seven or eight years, but I don't know if I can win a championship there." He also praised Patrick Ewing in a way that came across as criticism of James Donaldson.

The mood was so bad that Carter asked Motta to fly to Dallas and "build some bridges" that he'd damaged. Sonju was hoping Motta would call it a big misunderstanding and help get fans excited for next season. Motta said he didn't understand why everyone was so upset, pointing out that the Mavericks gave him permission to talk to other teams. (Carter did so as a good-faith gesture.)

Carter and Motta met for two hours on Monday, May 18, 1987. Carter said Motta apologized for anything that might've hurt the team. Motta called it a good meeting, but added that he wouldn't comment further until a Wednesday afternoon news conference. It was considered such a non-event that The Associated Press sent an intern and a radio station sent its newest reporter—without a tape recorder. But Motta walked into Carter's office 15 minutes before the gathering and said he was retiring. Carter was too stunned to respond. He didn't even warn Sonju and Rick Sund. They ended up finding out when everyone else did.

"I might have been able to talk with Dick and change him before we got to the press—if I could have thought straight," Carter later recalled. "I was numb going over there. I was empty coming back."

Motta smacked a wad of gum while reading his goodbye speech. It lasted one minute, 43 seconds, and he didn't take questions.

"Friendship is never having to say you're sorry," Motta said. "I was very ethical and also professional. Totally. And if the same circumstances ever arose again, I would do exactly the same thing. I cannot apologize for any of my actions or quotes.

"There will never be a job or position important enough in my lifetime to compromise my values or give up any part of my integrity. So, therefore, I am retiring as coach of the Dallas Mavericks."

Motta said "retire" instead of "resign" because that let him cash in on a pension plan Carter had set up.

HIRING A NEW COACH

Despite the recent mayhem, the Dallas job was a doozie. Who wouldn't want to coach a team that had just won 55 games and its division, had an average age of 26, and had a set lineup featuring proven scorers Mark Aguirre and Rolando Blackman, backcourt leader Derek Harper and a frontcourt of Sam Perkins, Roy Tarpley and Donaldson?

Don Nelson was already the front-runner when he resigned from the Milwaukee Bucks, a move as intriguing as Motta's departure in Dallas. Carter made no secret of the fact that Nelson was his only candidate. Nelson even said, "If I coach next year, it will be in Dallas."

While there was some question about the stiff compensation Milwaukee wanted, a bigger concern was getting him in for a formal interview. The Mavs were in a race with the Golden State Warriors, who were owned by Nelson's friend Jim Fitzgerald. The holdup: Fitzgerald was in Ireland.

Then things got weird again. Nelson told Dallas no and went to Golden State as a part owner. He then told the Mavericks they couldn't interview Warriors coach George Karl. Former Philadelphia coach Billy Cunningham also told the Mavs he wasn't interested. Another popular candidate was San Antonio coach Bob Weiss, Motta's former assistant. But the Spurs wanted compensation, and the Mavericks were only willing to give something up for Nelson. Boston assistant Jimmy Rodgers was out because he, too, likely would've required compensation.

That left two options: assistant coach Richie Adubato and John MacLeod, who'd been fired by Phoenix in February after 13 years with the franchise.

The knock on Adubato was a lack of experience. In his only NBA coaching stint, he went 12-58 after replacing Dick Vitale with the Pistons in 1979-80. While he knew the town and the team, there were doubts about whether he could get the most out of this rising team.

That made MacLeod the safe choice. He'd won at least 50 games four times in Phoenix and took a 42-40 team to the NBA Finals in 1976. The knock against him was that he didn't always get along with his top veterans—and Dallas didn't need any problems between a new coach and Aguirre.

Sund and Sonju met with MacLeod for two days, then enthusiastically recommended him to Carter. MacLeod wanted the Dallas job enough that he canceled an interview with the Knicks. That was significant because their new general manager, Al Bianchi, had been his assistant in Phoenix.

MacLeod's candidacy was endorsed by the man who fired him in Phoenix, Jerry Colangelo, and by Lakers GM Jerry West. Motta was in favor, too. Carter, though, still had other candidates in mind when he flew to Phoenix to meet MacLeod. He didn't when he left, however, and on June 4, 1987, MacLeod became the second coach in team history.

"I won't be in a situation where I'm continually worrying about how I measure up to Dick," MacLeod said at a news conference. "Dick is gone now. And I'm the new coach. I'm not going to look over my shoulder. I'm going to look forward."

There was one Motta tradition he upheld right away—a handshake deal with Carter instead of a signed contract.

Adubato remained the top assistant. Gar Heard joined him and Clifford Ray was hired to work with the big men. Nelson, meanwhile, spent a year as executive vice president of the Warriors, then fired Karl and named himself coach.

1987 DRAFT: FARMER AND ALFORD

Jim Farmer joined the list of bad draft choices when Dallas took him 20th in the 1987 draft. Nobody taken that low should be considered a huge flop, yet he's often lumped with Bill Garnett in discussions about worst first-round picks. (The better choice at 20th would've been Reggie Lewis, who went 22nd to Boston and became a star before dying of a heart problem.)

Farmer played 30 games in Dallas, then went to the CBA and Italy. He resurfaced in Nashville in 2003 trying to make it as a country music singer.

Dallas used the third pick of the second round on Steve Alford. Released and re-signed several times, he played a total of 112 games in Dallas over four seasons. His unique distinction in team history is having played the most games without starting. He also provided a hilarious scene on January 23, 1990, when he went into a game with his shorts on backwards.

"I've been praying for more attention," Alford said. "I now know I have to be more specific."

MacLEOD PICKS UP WHERE MOTTA LEFT OFF

A three-pointer by Harper with one second left made MacLeod a winner in his Mavs debut. And things got better from there.

Dallas led the Midwest Division from late December to mid-April, padded by a franchise-record 11-game winning streak. A bid for consecutive division titles ended on the second to last day of the season. Still, the Mavs finished with 53 wins, one less than Denver, and went into the playoffs as the third seed.

Regular-season highlights included Blackman scoring his 10,000[th] career point and MacLeod earning his 600th career win.

But there were many additional honors that season.

Aguirre and Donaldson were All-Stars. It was extra special for Aguirre because the game was in his hometown of Chicago— and because he got married the day before the game. Isiah Thomas, Magic Johnson and future Maverick Herb Williams were all part of the ceremony.

Roy Tarpley was named Sixth Man of the Year, making him the first Maverick to win a major leaguewide honor. Tarpley averaged 11.8 rebounds in 28.5 minutes per game. He finished seventh in the league in rebounding, making him the first non-starter ever to crack the top 10. For the second straight year, he averaged the most rebounds per minute in the league.

Coach John MacLeod inherited a 50-win team that featured a lineup of Roy Tarpley, Mark Aguirre, Rolando Blackman, Sam Perkins and Derek Harper. (NBAE/Getty Images)

He was named Player of the Week in late February after averaging 17.3 points and 16.8 rebounds for the previous four games, then responded with 16 points and 21 rebounds his next game.

"You can coach a long time and never have a player as dominant in one area as Roy is [in rebounding]," MacLeod said. "I'm just glad he's on our side."

Before the season, Tarpley admitted to having received professional help for a drug problem. That put him into the league's drug program, which meant frequent testing and ongoing aftercare treatment. He essentially was on probation, because a second "strike" would result in suspension. His mother moved to Dallas to help take care of him, and Carter often joined him for therapy sessions.

Yet another honor was the gushing headline "Dallas' Backcourt Is the NBA's Best!" that accompanied a cover photo of

Rolando Blackman and Derek Harper in the March 1988 issue of *Basketball Digest.* A subheadline summed up the premise of the article: "Some guards are individually better (Magic, Jordan), but no backcourt combo can match this prototype duo in Dallas."

The Lakers' PR director showed the magazine to Johnson and Byron Scott before tipoff of a March 6 matchup. Their response came through loud and clear: Scott scored 28 points in a 108-97 victory at Reunion, ending Dallas's 11-game winning streak. Scott had 35 a week later in Los Angeles, but the Mavericks won 110-101. The Lakers won the next meeting 114-107 behind a Reunion Arena-record 23 assists by Johnson. (When Utah's Rickey Green had a building-best 17 in 1985, he said, "Doesn't Magic Johnson come in here?")

THE GREATEST POSTSEASON

ROUND ONE: AGUIRRE GOES B-O-N-K-E-R-S

By scoring 43 points in the fourth quarter of a Game 1 victory over Houston during the 1987-88 playoffs, the Mavericks began erasing the memories of the previous postseason.

Game 2, however, brought back some of those sickening feelings as Sleepy Floyd and Hakeem Olajuwon joined Elgin Baylor and Jerry West as the only teammates to each score 40 in a playoff game.

Dallas regained control of the series by winning Game 3. Then came the third quarter of Game 4, possibly the best 12 minutes ever played by a Maverick.

Aguirre, who had been benched during key moments of earlier games in the series, made 10 of 11 shots for 27 points in the period. His only miss was a three-pointer, but he made three others from behind the arc. Aguirre finished with 38 points, and Dallas advanced to the second round.

"Mark went B-O-N-K-E-R-S," Perkins said.

Blackman was happy to put the Seattle series behind the team.

"We got the monkey off our back—the gorilla, the bear, whatever animal you call it," he said. "The monkey is dead ... clubbed to death."

BRING ON THE LAKERS!

The Denver Nuggets were next, and they beat Dallas in the opener by 11. The Mavericks won Game 2 by 14, marking the first time in eight meetings all season that a road team had won.

Back at Reunion Arena for Game 3, Dallas led from start to ... almost finish. Bill Hanzlik tied the game with a 10-foot jumper with 35 seconds left, then made a layup with three seconds left for Denver's only lead—and the only one that mattered. Fat Lever had a triple double (11 points, 11 rebounds and 14 assists) as Denver went up 2-1 in the series. But Lever strained a knee in the game and didn't return. Old friend Jay Vincent, now with the Nuggets, also had a pulled calf muscle and missed the rest of the series.

The Mavericks capitalized, winning the next three games. Aguirre scored 24 in a 21-point victory in Game 4, then sank a three-pointer with 19 seconds left to win Game 5. In the capper, Blackman scored seven points in a late 10-2 run, and Tarpley added 18 points and 19 rebounds, sending Dallas to the conference finals for the first time in franchise history.

THE WESTERN CONFERENCE FINALS

The Mavericks were four wins from reaching the NBA Finals. Then three. Then two. Then one.

The Lakers won Game 1 by 15 points, then had it even easier in Game 2 as they made 62 percent of their shots. Back in Dallas, the Mavericks trailed by one going into the fourth quarter of Game 3, but won by 12. Tarpley finished with 21 points and 20 rebounds, and Aguirre had 23 points and 10 rebounds. Harper scored 35 in Game 4, a 14-point Dallas win, to send the series back to Los Angeles all knotted up.

Game 5 was a lot like the others at the Forum, as the Lakers won big. But back in Dallas, the Mavericks won a thrilling Game 6. In the final 33 seconds, Tarpley stripped James Worthy on a possible tying layup; then Donaldson blocked a Worthy layup.

About 500 fans showed up at the airport to send the team off in style for the flight to Los Angeles. They were still clinging to hope during Game 7 as the Mavericks were within one point at halftime, down only 76-74 late in the third quarter, and behind just 100-94 with 5:34 left.

But the Lakers wouldn't crack. A 17-2 run started by a Worthy dunk and a tip-in by Kareem Abdul-Jabbar sent Los Angeles to a 117-102 victory. The Lakers went on to beat the Pistons in the finals to become the first repeat champions since the 1968-69 Boston Celtics.

"It was so close," Carter said, "you could taste it."

More than 4,000 fans were waiting for the Mavericks at the airport when the team returned from Los Angeles.

"None of us will forget that tremendous show of support," Sund said.

While sad that the season was over, everyone was excited about the future. Nobody would've believed that Dallas wouldn't win another playoff game until April 28, 2001.

SECTION II:

The Gory Days

(JUNE 5, 1988 TO DECEMBER 4, 1997)

9

From One Mess to Another

AGUIRRE'S ACHING HAND

It's hard to call this the beginning of the end, but it sure was ominous. Early in the fourth quarter of Game 7 against the Lakers, Mark Aguirre bent back two fingers on his left hand, aggravating a knuckle injury. He'd scored 11 points in the third quarter, and the Mavericks needed him on the court, even as a decoy.

But Aguirre sat and iced his fingers, a reminder of two other injury absences in the late minutes of big games against the Lakers: a hip problem in Game 4 in 1984 and ankle pain in Game 6 in '86.

This time, the Mavericks were down by eight when Aguirre went to the bench. They were down nine when he returned 2:53 later, with 8:45 left. Aguirre scored only two more points and later said his hand was "no problem." Fans generally remember him being out longer, returning with less time remaining and the deficit growing by more. Even owner Donald Carter seemed to think Aguirre's absence was the difference.

Years later, Carter said that if Dick Motta had still been the coach, he would've pulled out a pocketknife and offered to cut off anything that hurt. Carter believed Aguirre would've gone back in and the Mavericks would have won the game and the series, then beaten Detroit for the title, as the Lakers did.

Under MacLeod, though, the Mavericks held a mandatory team meeting in Dallas a few days into the off season. The only player missing: Mark Aguirre.

FIRST-ROUND ABSENCE

After years of gathering first-round draft picks, Dallas went without one for the first time in 1988.

The Mavericks gave this choice—the 20th—to Miami to avoid losing Uwe Blab, Bill Wennington and Steve Alford in the expansion draft.

"We're going into our ninth season, and in these past playoffs we came within a few minutes of getting into the NBA Finals," GM Norm Sonju said. "Our coaches and basketball people feel that the bench players on our team are important to our success."

Another part of the deal with the Heat that's worth remembering is the wonderful name Arvid Kramer, the player Miami actually selected from Dallas. Kramer was a 6-foot-10 center who played eight games for Denver in 1979-80. The Mavericks acquired him through their dispersal draft—the start of their quest for a big man?—but he opted to play in Europe, so they still had his rights.

For what it's worth, he never showed up in Miami, either.

THE CRUMBLING BEGINS

Nobody knew. How could they?

In the summer of 1988, the Mavericks were gearing up for their most anticipated season yet. They'd been within a win of the NBA Finals, and everyone was coming back. By December 29, Dallas was 17-9, leading the Western Conference.

Then the Mavericks lost 11 of 15, including seven straight. Everything that could go wrong did. There were injuries. A suspension. A trade of a star player who wanted to leave Dallas for a star player who had no interest in coming. The expected starting five wound up playing together only twice all season.

Dallas finished at 38-44, the first losing record in six years. Despite it all, the Mavs were in the playoff race until the 1,025th and final game of the NBA season—a Portland-Sacramento matchup that went into overtime. The Blazers won, earning the eighth and final seed.

AGUIRRE: THE FINAL ACT

Aguirre was tired of playing in Dallas, and the Mavericks were tired of having him around. He began forcing his way out in December 1988 by refusing to go into a game during the fourth quarter. Two nights later, Aguirre headed to the bench with five fouls, walked past coach John MacLeod, cussed and extended his middle finger. MacLeod said he didn't see the gesture. Aguirre said it was directed at press row.

Four nights after Carter told Aguirre—and the entire team—to expect a trade soon, Aguirre warmed up to play Utah, even going one on one with Derek Harper. He then went into the locker room, declared his ankles were sore and missed the game. After Dallas lost by 15, his feet looked fine as he scooted past a pack of reporters.

"It's a beautiful night outside, man," he said, smiling. "This is really a trip. Have a good day and all that kind of stuff. I really got to get going, fellas. Sorry."

The scene left plenty of questions about the legitimacy of his injury—especially when he scored 36 points the next game. He had 16 points in the third quarter of the game after that, then became lazy in the fourth period. MacLeod benched Aguirre without making a fuss.

Aguirre's most curious performance came in the next game. He played 14 minutes in the second half and took only one shot while hardly giving any effort on either end of the court. Dallas blew a 16-point lead to Portland—a loss that ultimately allowed the Blazers to edge the Mavericks for a playoff spot.

Just when everyone wanted to be done with him, Aguirre scored 32 in the last game before the All-Star break. In the first game back, he had 29 points, nine assists and five rebounds.

The next day, Aguirre's phone rang at 9:15 a.m. It was Rick Sund was on the other end, calling to say Aguirre was now a Detroit Piston. It was exactly what he wanted. Aguirre was reunited with close friend Isiah Thomas and was heading to a team that just went to the NBA Finals and appeared on its way back. And indeed they would go back, winning the title that year and the next.

"Today should be an all-day party because he's gone," Sam Perkins said. "Good luck, Detroit, because you're going to need it."

Aguirre didn't go to the airport alone. He shared a ride with Carter, who was headed to Seattle. And guess who was waiting to greet Aguirre with the Pistons? Their television analyst, Dick Motta.

The two ex-Mavericks faced Dallas for the first time on March 27 in Detroit. After the Pistons won, Motta interviewed Aguirre about how strange it was.

"I was out there watching them run their plays, and I was thinking, 'Hey, the guy sitting over there taught me those plays,'" Aguirre said.

"Yeah," Motta interjected, "and if you would have run them the way I taught you, your scoring average would have been up where it should have been."

Aguirre left Dallas with plenty of team records, including the most points, rebounds and starts. And the most hard feelings created.

ADRIAN DANTLEY: ANOTHER MESS

The deal for Aguirre brought Dallas a first-round pick in 1991 and Adrian Dantley, the 10th leading scorer in NBA history and the leading scorer against the Mavericks.

Dantley also had been traded four times before in his 13-year career, so he knew the drill. Only this time, he was upset. Furious. He was in no mood to report to Dallas. So he didn't.

While Dantley never said it, his anger apparently was aimed at Thomas for lobbying team owner Bill Davidson to make the move. Dantley was leading the team in scoring, but Thomas wanted his buddy Aguirre, and the front office gave in.

After two days of waiting for Dantley, the Mavericks could've vetoed the deal. Instead, they told Dantley he'd be fined for every game he missed. They eventually let the rest of the league know he could be had for a first-round pick.

During his holdout, Dantley appeard on the CBS game of the week to be interviewed by his friend Brent Musburger. Much to the chagrin of team officials, Dantley told a national TV audience he was "screwed," a term that was considered vulgar in 1989.

The Mavericks told Dantley he'd be suspended if he didn't show up by February 23, the trade deadline. He flew in at 10 p.m. and held a news conference.

"I'm sincerely happy to be here," Dantley said. "I felt I couldn't come in the beginning because I wasn't ready to play basketball. The circumstances were so unusual, I just needed to sort things out."

In keeping with the turbulent storyline, Dantley's debut was the worst home loss in team history, a 127-92 whipping by Golden State. Dantley contributed by going 0 for seven and committing a team-worst five turnovers.

"I felt like a rookie," he said.

He redeemed himself the next game, going 11 of 13 from the field and 10 of 10 from the foul line for 32 points in 29 minutes of a 127-93 victory—a 34-point win following a 35-point loss.

It came against the Bullets, which meant it was shown on local TV in Washington, where Dantley's family lived. But only die-hard Mavericks fans even noticed. That same day, Jerry Jones bought the Dallas Cowboys and fired Tom Landry.

When the Mavericks and Pistons met in Detroit a few weeks later, Dantley whispered something to Thomas just before tipoff. While neither repeated what was said, it certainly wasn't "Good to see you."

THE ROY TARPLEY BLOTTER

The timeline of Mavericks history is being interrupted for details of the Roy Tarpley saga because, well, franchise history was interrupted by the Tarpley saga. It fits here because it was during the 1988-89 season that Tarpley's problems became overwhelming.

Can one player matter that much? Consider "The Tarpley Effect."

Year	With	Without	Comment
1986-87	51-24	4-3	Made All-Rookie team
1987-88	52-29	1-0	Strike 1 in preseason; Sixth Man of the Year
1988-89	12-7	26-37	Knee injury (14 g), suspended (strike 2; 49 g)
1989-90	29-16	18-19	Suspended twice (33g, 2 g.)
1990-91	4-1	24-53	Season-ending knee surgery; suspension
1991-92	—	22-60	Strike 3 in preseason; banned
1992-93	—	11-71	Banned
1993-94	—	13-69	Banned
1994-95	27-28	9-18	Knee injury, suspension

Totals:
With: 175-105(.625)
Without: 128-330 (.279)

Tarpley was the perfect player in the perfect place at the perfect time. Problem was, Tarpley wasn't perfect. Far from it.

With power forward extraordinaire Roy Tarpley (left) and James Donaldson (right), the Mavericks had two solid seven-footers. Tarpley's drug problems left Mavericks fans wondering what might've been. (NBAE/Getty Images)

Maybe he was a victim of his own addictive demons, or simply unable to handle success. Whatever. The bottom line is that his life, career and team all fell apart at the same time.

Tarpley never made it to the prime of his career, at least not the way he should have. The Mavericks knew Tarpley used drugs in college, but hoped he'd be clean as a pro. Instead he got his first strike in the league's drug program after his rookie season, and the second came early in his third season. After a series of suspensions that essentially counted as foul balls, he drew a third strike in October 1991 when he refused to take a drug test. The league imposed a minimum two-year ban on Tarpley. He was eligible to apply for reinstatement in October 1993, but he waited until May 1994. He rejoined the team in October 1994; 14 months later he was banned again.

When he left for good, Tarpley was fifth on the team's all-time list in rebounds and blocks, sixth in steals and eighth in points—despite playing only 280 games. That's the equivalent of less than three seasons. He started only 57 times.

"[Tarpley] had the combination of fluidity, talent, skill, and the nastiness to command the position—not play it, command it," Rolando Blackman said. "With his outside jumper and rebounding presence, he could've had 25 points and 17 rebounds every night. Losing him devastated us completely. We lost the power piece we needed to win."

Here's a breakdown of his troubles:

• November 16-December 14, 1988—Missed 14 games with a knee injury.

• January 5-April 11, 1989—Suspended for violating league's drug policy a second time.

• October 27, 1989—Fined $250 for missing a practice; couldn't be located for nearly 24 hours.

• November 15, 1989 to January 22, 1990—Arrested for driving while intoxicated and resisting arrest, leading to a 33-game suspension.

• March 10, 1990—Fined $250 for missing a team flight to Houston.

- March 30, 1990—Fined $250 for missing a pregame walkthrough.
- April 6, 1990—Suspended for two games and fined $250 for missing practice.
- November 9, 1990—Season-ending knee injury.
- March 30, 1991—Indefinite suspension following arrest on suspicion of drunk driving.
- May 5, 1991—Arrested in Houston for allegedly assaulting a woman claiming to be his girlfriend.
- October 16, 1991—Strike three. Banned for at least two years.
- May 20, 1994—Applied for reinstatement.
- September 30, 1994—Reinstated.
- October 6, 1994—Signs $25.8 million, six-year contract.
- October 29, 1994—Ticketed for driving 92 mph on the North Dallas Tollway at 2:50 a.m. An hour later, his Mercedes strikes a utility pole and is abandoned.
- November 17, 1994—Tarpley plays first NBA game in four years.
- December 13-15, 1994—Sent home from a game for arguing with Motta, then suspended from the next game.
- January 27-February 28, 1995—Knee problems lead to month-long stay on injured list.
- June 24, 1995—Exposed in expansion draft, but not taken by Toronto or Vancouver.
- November 2-6, 1995—Unable to complete a physical because of a pancreas ailment.
- December 6, 1995—Banned again, this time for good.

During the summer of 2003, Tarpley reportedly asked the league to reinstate him again. If reinstated, the Mavs would own his rights. However, it is unlikely that any team, including Dallas, would be interested in a 38-year-old player nearly a decade removed from the NBA.

10

The Last Gasp

MAILMAN II? SHOULD'VE BEEN "RETURN TO SENDER"

The similarities were striking. Dallas had the eighth pick of the draft. There was a power forward coming out of Louisiana Tech who impressed the scouts. In 1985, the Mavericks bypassed Karl Malone. In 1989, they were determined not to make the same mistake twice. So they drafted Randy White, or, as *Sports Illustrated* dubbed him, "Mailman II."

White was 6-foot-7, 255 pounds—roughly the same size as Malone. Both were from small towns and were close to mothers named Shirley. White had spent several summers working out with Malone, and he moved to Dallas months before the draft to play pickup games against NBA players. He even had the same Dallas-based agent Malone had when he was drafted.

White was considered a bit unpolished, but optimists considered that room for improvement. There also were whispers that the Mavericks needed another power forward because of looming uncertainty about Tarpley. Oh, there was the name thing, too. One of the best and most popular players in Dallas Cowboys history was named Randy White.

"He's got some big shoes to fill if he's going to live up to the name of Randy White in Dallas," Mavs owner Donald Carter said. "If he can do for us what a Randy White has done before in this town, praise the Lord."

White turned out to be more awkward than dominant. The only time he was fun to watch was during his frequent stays on the injured list; a sharp dresser, he showed off his extensive wardrobe while sitting courtside.

He played five seasons in Dallas, was released, and never latched on elsewhere. His career averages: 7.4 points and 4.9 rebounds.

Meanwhile, the guy some Mavericks insiders suggested be drafted instead of White became an All-Star in Golden State. His name is Tim Hardaway, and he gets added to the list of could've beens.

MacLEOD FIRED; ADUBATO PROMOTED

Carter thought about firing coach John MacLeod at the All-Star break in February 1989. However, he ended up leaving MacLeod in charge at the start of the 1989-90 season.

In November, during the second half of a 47-point loss to Seattle that remains the worst spanking at home in team history, fans chanted, "John must go!" Three days later, they got their wish.

"The Mavericks have a multitude of problems," said Rick Sund, by this time the vice president of basketball operations. "We want to address those problems one at a time. Certainly John has not caused those problems, but at this particular time, in order to get the team turned around, we feel a coaching change is necessary."

Assistant coach Richie Adubato took over with the Mavs at 5-6. They went 42-29 the rest of the season and made the playoffs.

"We have a great respect for Richie as a coach, and as a person he cares about us," said Rolando Blackman, who made his fourth All-Star team. "He knows the game, and we respect his judgment."

ONE LAST BREATH OF FRESH AIR

The Mavericks made their only playoff trip in the 1990s during the 1989-90 season and had some memorable games along the way. There was the first triple-overtime game in team history, a 144-140 loss to Portland in which James Donaldson played 58 minutes, still the team record. And there was a 106-93 victory over the Dick Motta-coached Sacramento Kings in late January.

But the top highlight came on March 25, a night that was emotionally charged from the start because it was Mark Aguirre's first time in Reunion Arena since being traded to Detroit. The Pistons were defending NBA champions, had the league's best record, and a week before had beaten the Mavs by 30.

Fans gave Aguirre the Kiki Vandeweghe treatment. He was booed when he was introduced and every time he touched the ball, but responded with 14 points in 26 minutes.

The Pistons led by nine with 7:25 left. Then Derek Harper got rolling. He scored eight points in the closing minutes, including a 20-footer with 23 seconds left that forced overtime. He made a three-pointer and a layup in the final 16.8 seconds of overtime to win by two.

"It's the greatest comeback victory I've ever been associated with, and that's 30 years of coaching," Adubato said.

This was one of 15 games Dallas won when trailing at the start of the fourth period. The previous best was eight, so that says something about this group's resilience. This also was the 10th season in team history. The first decade ended with a respectable record of 405-415.

ADIOS, A.D.

Adrian Dantley and the Mavericks were never a good fit. It was a forced marriage, prompted by the team's need to divorce Aguirre. Before the one-year anniversary, both sides wanted out. So in January 1990, Dantley agreed to become a free agent after the season. He was thrilled to be leaving, saying he never felt wanted. The Mavs were excited about saving $1.2 million.

But Dantley's tenure ended even sooner than expected. On February 3, he knocked knees with Portland's Terry Porter, broke a bone in his right leg, and never suited up for Dallas again. Although team doctors cleared him to return in April, he didn't want to risk it. He had no problem with being left off the playoff roster.

Over 76 games with the Mavericks, Dantley averaged 17 points. He didn't play another game until April 1991, joining Milwaukee for 10 regular-season games and three more in the playoffs. Then his NBA career was over.

1990 PLAYOFFS: SWEPT AWAY

After a one-year playoff absence, the Mavericks went to Portland seeking their first postseason victory since Game 6 of the 1988 Western Conference finals. They finished the series still searching for it.

The Blazers used a late 9-0 run to win the opener, then Dallas blew an early 15-point lead in Game 2, partly because Steve Alford couldn't defend backup guards Drazen Petrovic or Danny Young in the second quarter.

Game 3 was at Reunion Arena, marking the only playoff game there in the '90s. Despite Buck Williams leaving in the first quarter with cuts around his eye and Kevin Duckworth breaking a hand late in the third quarter, the Blazers still won by 14—their largest margin of victory during the series.

What made this series-ending loss so frustrating was that Tarpley failed to take advantage of Portland being without its big men. But Tarpley wasn't his usual self, either. His first field goal came midway through the third quarter, and it took a goaltending call to get it. He went two of 12 from the field and two of eight on free throws, finishing with six points—16 less than he averaged the first two games. He also had five turnovers.

He blamed his performance on lingering effects of an upset stomach caused by spicy fried chicken and jalapeno peppers from a fast-food restaurant. After all his other vices that had hurt the team, it was his appetite that doomed the Mavericks this time.

SO LONG, SAM

In 1989, Sam Perkins asked for a $10 million, five-year contract. But the Mavericks were concerned that his knees wouldn't hold up that long, so they countered with $5.1 million over three years.

They ended up settling on a one-year contract for $975,000, setting the stage for another round of negotiations and the risk that he'd leave as a free agent.

By April 1990, the Mavericks upped their offer to $18 million for six years. But Perkins, who had overtaken Aguirre as the franchise's leading rebounder, opted to shop around. In August, Perkins's agent said he had a $20 million offer and asked Dallas to match it.

GM Norm Sonju was vacationing in Austria when he got the ultimatum. He didn't like the threat and wasn't keen on going up another $2 million, especially considering that Perkins failed to keep the team afloat in Tarpley's absences. After talking to owner Donald Carter, Sonju sent Perkins and his agent a letter saying they wouldn't match it. They also wished him well if he left.

"I was ready to forget everything that happened," Perkins said a few weeks later, "until that letter came."

But Perkins didn't get $20 million. He signed with the Lakers for $19.2 million, which was less than Dallas's final offer when factoring in California's higher cost of living and state income tax, which Texas doesn't have. While Perkins's fiscal logic seemed flawed, he was still set for life. And he was joining the Lakers, which meant playing alongside Magic Johnson and James Worthy, virtually guaranteeing that he'd be in the championship race for many years.

For Mavs fans, losing Perkins was bad enough. Seeing him in Lakers yellow only made it worse.

Perkins played 11 more seasons with Los Angeles, Seattle and Indiana. He made the finals with all three teams, but never won a championship.

11

Going for Broke

A GOOD IDEA AT THE TIME ...

The Mavericks had a decision to make: Rebuild for the first time or reload for one more championship bid with their remaining core players—Rolando Blackman, Derek Harper and Roy Tarpley?

They opted for the quick fix.

In June 1990, Dallas sent two first-round picks to Denver for Fat Lever, an All-Star the last two seasons. Two more first-rounders went to Sacramento for Rodney McCray. After losing Perkins, the Mavericks signed Alex English; it was hailed as the best free agent signing in team history.

The plan was for Blackman, Harper and Lever to lead a three-guard attack, with a frontcourt rotation featuring Tarpley, McCray, English, James Donaldson and Herb Williams, who'd been acquired in 1989 for Detlef Schrempf.

Some ranked the Mavericks as a championship contender. The roster was even called their best ever.

... *TURNS INTO THE NEXT MAJOR MISSTEP*

A 4-1 start turned into a 6-7 record, and the Mavericks never recovered. A season-worst 34-point loss in the season finale left Dallas with just 28 wins, the fewest since the second season.

Lever and Tarpley were both lost to season-ending knee injuries after just five games. English averaged 9.7 points, his worst mark since his rookie season, and ended up retiring. McCray was solid with 11.4 points and 7.6 rebounds, but this team needed more than solid.

With the future already mortgaged, there was little for fans to look forward to—no rookies to give extended minutes, nothing left to trade and a big chunk of the salary cap promised to Tarpley. It's no wonder that Rick Sund, who put the roster together, was loudly booed at the home finale.

Among the few highlights was Blackman passing Mark Aguirre as the franchise's leading scorer and Harper becoming the first player in league history to increase his scoring average in his first eight seasons. English became the seventh player to go over 25,000 career points and Williams joined the 10,000-point club, but those feats only served as reminders of what those players once were.

There was some satisfaction in beating the John MacLeod-coached Knicks in his first game back at Reunion Arena. And Dallas was involved in two history-making games: Dick Motta-coached Sacramento losing its record-tying 28th consecutive road game and Magic Johnson passing Oscar Robertson as the career assist leader.

A WIN COSTS DALLAS SHAQ—NO FOOLIN'

The '91-92 season was off to a bad start even before Dallas lost the first three games. Tarpley was banned during training camp, leaving no time to find a replacement. Even though his $8.45 million, three-year deal was voided, where can you find a

26-year-old power forward capable of averaging 20 points and 10 rebounds?

Without Tarpley, the Mavericks were an old team going no-where. All five starters and two key reserves were over 30. Top draft pick Doug Smith held out, then started slowly. Brad Davis suffered a career-ending back injury. Donaldson got into a fight at practice that led to a suspension, then a trade for the forget-table Brian Quinnett. Lever was lost to another knee injury after 31 games. There were losing streaks of eight, 11 and 15 games, plus a club-record 26 straight losses on the road. The Mavericks finished 22-60, averaging 97.6 points—fewest in the NBA and in team history.

Among the few highlights was the way they celebrated the 100th anniversary of the day Dr. James Naismith nailed a peach basket to a gymnasium wall and invented what he called "basket ball." Dallas beat the Kings 109-85 for the most lopsided win of the season. It also gave Motta his 856th career loss, the most ever for a coach.

Among the lowlights was the team blowing a 26-point lead, a collapse made even more spectacular by the fact that Dallas scored 71 points in the first half, then just 34 in the second half.

Yet the worst thing that happened all season was one of the victories. On April 1—yep, April Fool's Day—the Mavs beat the Orlando Magic 102-89 at Reunion Arena. No big deal at the time turned out to be huge news after the draft lottery. Because the Magic had one more loss than Dallas, they also had a few more ping-pong balls. One of them wound up being selected No. 1, which gave Orlando the pick used to draft Shaquille O'Neal.

Maybe it's oversimplifying things to say that if the Magic had won on April 1 then the Mavericks would have Shaquille O'Neal. But it's another of those "What ifs?" that makes fans gnash their teeth.

12

The Mav-Wrecks

1992 DRAFT: THE FIRST "J" ARRIVES

After all the thrills Rolando Blackman provided, he'd earned the right to get away from the mess the Mavericks had become. Blackman almost was dealt in February 1992, when teams would've given up plenty for a proven scorer. Instead, Dallas waited until draft day, getting only a first-round pick in 1995 from the Knicks, the team he rooted for while growing up in Brooklyn.

Hours later, the Mavericks replaced their all-time leading scorer by taking Jim Jackson with the fourth overall pick. Jackson fit the Blackman mold—he was a shooting guard who was respected on and off the court. They even wore the same number, 22.

Jackson scored brownie points when he came to town the next day and said that out of respect for Blackman he'd take another number. He requested 24. The last No. 24? Mark Aguirre. It was a sign of things to come.

As for No. 22, the Mavericks finally retired it on March 11, 2000.

"I didn't make it here alone," Blackman said during a halftime ceremony in which the team retired his jersey. "I had help along the way."

Blackman spent two injury-marred seasons in New York, then played overseas for two years. He returned to Kansas State to continue his education and worked as a college basketball broadcaster.

Blackman returned to Dallas as an assistant coach in 2000-01. When the playoffs approached at the end of that season, he considered a comeback. Plans were scrubbed when he tore his Achilles tendon.

"Not a lot of people can shoot a jumper any more, so I was thinking about giving myself a viable chance to be a force on the court," Blackman said. "It wasn't about my glory, it was about helping the team win."

THE MAV-WRECKS

With Blackman gone and Jackson holding out for 54 games, the Mavericks celebrated the 20th anniversary of the Philadelphia 76ers' nine-win season by challenging that futility mark in 1992-93.

Dallas opened the season with two rookies in the lineup for the first time. In a telling statement about the quality of the roster, neither was a first-round pick. Sean Rooks was a second-rounder and Walter Bond was an undrafted free agent. (Later in the season, Morlon Wiley started while on a 10-day contract, another sad franchise first.)

Derek Harper wasn't pleased about still being around, then really was disappointed to last through the trade deadline.

The most embarrassing night, maybe in team history, came in late December when Dallas lost to lottery-bound Sacramento by 58. It's still the most lopsided loss—by 10.

Coach Richie Adubato was fired January 13 before a morning shootaround in Detroit. Assistant coach Gar Heard took over, and the Mavericks lost to the Pistons that night, dropping their record to 2-28. Quinn Buckner was interviewed the next day and became the top candidate. While other candidates were in-terviewed, Heard remained in charge. He even kept his job after Buckner was hired, a bizarre dynamic explained later during this chapter.

As the season wound down, the Mavericks were stuck at nine wins with two games left. Dallas beat Minnesota in the home finale, then headed to Houston for the final game. Heard wanted to go out in style, and the players responded. Forced to play a four-guard lineup because their four best big men were all in-jured, the Mavericks turned a 17-point deficit into a five-point win with a playing style guard Mike Iuzzolino describes as "a little bit of helter-skelter."

Dallas finished the season 11-71, the third worst record in NBA history. The Mavericks lost their first 29 road games. In that stretch, they probably would've done just as well by pulling 12 guys out of the stands, considering the paid professionals on their roster lost those games by an average of 21.8 points.

Making it all even worse was the fact that the Cowboys were on the way back up. When national media flocked to Dallas to chronicle their rise, reporters often stopped by Reunion to file stories about the Mavericks' demise.

Sports Illustrated ran an article under the headline "Comedy Club." *The Sporting News* poked fun by running mug shots of players without their names, challenging readers to put together names like Radisav Curcic with their pictures.

THE ARRIVAL OF JIM AND QUINN: 54 GAMES LATE AND 28 GAMES EARLY

Reporters arrived at Reunion Arena on March 4 to meet the coach of the 1993-94 Dallas Mavericks, which was strange enough considering there were 28 games left in the '92-93 season.

After Buckner was introduced, several of the first questions were about Jackson. Buckner stumbled over his answers, and there was some nervous laughter. Then a door opened and out walked the team's other new hire—Jackson.

Surprise!

JACKSON'S JOURNEY: 253 DAYS FROM SELECTION TO SIGNING

When Jackson was drafted, he told owner Donald Carter he wanted to be signed before training camp. It would take months for them to agree on anything again.

Things went wrong from the start. When Jackson visited Dallas the day after the draft, he held a news conference at Reunion Arena, then was told that GM Norm Sonju, vice president Rick Sund and coach Richie Adubato had other obligations. They offered for an assistant coach to take Jackson and his agent, Mark Termini, to dinner, but the pair opted to catch the next flight home.

The Mavs made their first contract offer in late July. Based on what the last two No. 4 picks received, Dallas offered $13.75 million over five years. Two months later, Termini counter-offered with $22.8 million over six years. When that turned out to be more than No. 3 pick Christian Laettner got, Termini went down to $21 million.

Training camp came and went without a deal. By opening day, neither side had budged. Realizing Dallas's last really good first-round pick was Tarpley in '86, Carter was hesitant to tie up so much money for so long in one player. He also was upholding the commissioner's suggestion that owners cut back on the long-term, high-dollar contracts they were giving to unproven rookies. While his stance was admirable, it was bad for business, considering other owners weren't doing it.

Carter also was stuck on the notion that guards don't deserve as much money as big men. Jackson countered by noting that the best players on the last four championship teams were guards—Michael Jordan in Chicago and Isiah Thomas in Detroit.

By mid-November, Jackson told Carter and Sonju he planned to go back to school if there was no progress soon. So on November 18, Carter, legal counsel Doug Adkins, Jackson and Termini met in Columbus, Ohio. They spent one hour on Carter's private jet, flying to Niagara Falls. They checked out the view from above, then returned to Columbus for lunch. During the trip, Jackson said he still wanted to be a Maverick, but the length of the deal remained a sticking point for him.

Soon after, Carter offered a $10.8 million, four-year deal that included $7 million for the first season. It was so poorly received that Carter's next move was giving Termini permission to attempt to set up a trade. Cleveland offered Danny Ferry, and the Mavericks laughed.

On December 11, the situation appeared irrevocably damaged when Jackson sent a fax—not to Carter, but to *The Dallas Morning News.* In three paragraphs, he blamed the team for "my rookie year to basically be ruined." And then there was this line: "I will not, under any circumstance, or at any time, play basketball for the Dallas Mavericks."

Carter sent a fax saying he was still hoping for a "win-win solution," but soon after revoked Termini's right to seek a trade. He said the team would do that for itself.

A flurry of activity at the trade deadline produced nothing. Jackson resigned himself to going back into the draft. Then Carter finally gave in. Within a week, they agreed on a $19 million, six-year deal, with the first year's salary set at $1.6 million and a $1 million signing bonus paid in full, despite two-thirds of the season being gone. Jackson signed the contract at the news conference in front of clicking cameras, 253 days after the Mavericks drafted him.

"I'm sorry it had to take so long," Jackson said. "But we're looking forward to the future, which is the most important thing right now. There's no need to dwell on the past."

So why did Carter change his mind?

"I'd like to know myself," he said.

THE YEAR THE MAVERICKS
REALLY WENT IN THE "TANK"

The preseason talk was about Dallas doubling its 11 wins from the previous season. Halfway through the season, the Mavericks were actually worse—just two wins, compared to three the year before. Even worse, they'd only beaten one team, Minnesota, which Buckner knew best because he spent the previous season as one of their broadcasters.

Dallas didn't win at Reunion Arena—not even against the Timberwolves—until January 29, the 42nd game. It was enough to earn the Mavericks three days of ridicule in the nationally syndicated comic strip "Tank McNamara."

In the first strip, the Mavs are shown coming out of the tunnel for pregame introductions wearing bags over their heads. Then Tank, a sportscaster, interviews one of the players, who says the team is so bad that opponents fear losing to them. "The biggest humiliation of your adult life," the opposing team's coach tells his club. In the final installment, the Mavericks pull off the upset victory, and one of the players pulls off his bag. He hands it to a player on the losing team and tells him, "You'll be needing this."

Here's the funniest part: Over the three days the strip ran, the Mavericks won twice. Their first winning streak of the season sent them into the All-Star break with six wins, putting the futility mark seemingly out of reach.

That is, until they lost every game in March. A 17-game losing streak ended with victory number nine. The Mavericks finished the year 13-69.

Thank goodness for the Timberwolves. Minnesota was the loser in six of Dallas's wins, including four of the first five. Although the Mavericks avoided setting a single-season futility record, their two-year mark of 24-140 is the worst in NBA history.

THE MIGHTY QUINN

Carter's negotiations with Buckner were the exact opposite of how he handled Jackson. Buckner asked for four years. Carter gave him five. The decision was part of Carter's new blind faith in Rick Sund. With this move, the leadership committee of Sund, Carter and Norm Sonju was history.

Sund had known Buckner for 17 years, since both were breaking in with the Milwaukee Bucks—Sund in the front office, Buckner on the court. Buckner, the first African-American hired to coach a pro team in Dallas, had been a leader and a winner his entire life. He won state championships his last two years in high school, was captain at Indiana for three seasons, including the undefeated national championship team in 1976, was captain of the U.S. Olympic team that won the gold medal in '76, and was on the Celtics teams that won the NBA title in 1984 and returned to the finals in '85. Among the coaches he'd played for were Bob Knight and Don Nelson. He was even an assistant to Knight on the 1984 U.S. Olympic team that won the gold medal in Los Angeles.

"I know I'm probably sticking my neck on the line with Quinn," Sund said. "But every time I watched Quinn Buckner play, he was coaching the game. The only difference is that he was playing, not on the sidelines coaching."

Buckner had the unique benefit of watching his team for the last third of the season before taking over. He already had been watching as an analyst for Minnesota Timberwolves broadcasts and on NBC's studio show, a job the Mavs let him keep through the playoffs. He came to games whenever he could, which made for an awkward scene. Reporters talked to interim coach Gar Heard, then got Buckner's reaction.

Quinn Buckner went 13-69 in his only season in charge. His winning percentage of .159 is among the worst in pro sports history.
(NBAE/Getty Images)

MORE LOUSY LOTTERY LUCK
TURNS INTO THE NEXT "J"

Despite having the worst record in the NBA, the Mavericks wound up with the fourth pick in the 1993 draft. That meant missing out on yet another franchise frontcourt player, Chris Webber. They ended up with Jamal Mashburn, a solid pick. The combination of him and Jackson sparked hopes of another high-scoring duo like Mark Aguirre and Blackman.

Mashburn actually was excited to be joining such a bad team because it meant more playing time.

"I just want to be part of an organization that's going to grow," he said.

Mashburn missed the first six days of training camp, but suited up in time for the first preseason game.

Did he get in so quickly because he took a four-year deal? Hardly. Mashburn got $34.8 million over *eight* years.

UNLUCKY AT LOTTO

No team has played the NBA lottery worse than Dallas.

Of the 13 times the Mavericks have been connected—either with their own pick, someone else's or someone else using their pick—only once has the number they've selected been a better seed than where they ended up ranking according to record. It's been worse five times, including the two years Dallas had the league's ugliest record, which in other sports would automatically earn the No. 1 choice.

Dallas has played the lottery in every form. The Mavs were there when it was seven teams, nine teams (which happened only once, 1989), 11 teams and 13 teams. They were there when every pick was up for grabs ('85-86) and plenty of times when only the top three choices were at stake ('87-present). They've also done the random selection of envelopes and the weighted method using ping-pong balls (first done using 66 balls, then 1,000). Dallas was even the reason for the added balls. The league realized it needed to weigh the system even more after the 1993 lottery, when the Mavericks, who had the worst record, picked fourth, while the Orlando Magic, which had the best record of any team in the pool, wound up first.

The following proves how unlucky Dallas has been. The "rank" category refers to where the Mavericks' record ranked among the league's worst the previous season. The "result" category refers to where the Mavericks ended up picking in the draft.

Year	Rank	Result	Comment
1986	3	7	Rank, result came from Cleveland
1989	8	8	
1990	8	3	Rank, result from Washington; traded to Denver for Fat Lever
1991	6	6	
1992	3	4	
1993	1	4	
1994	1	2	
1995	10	12	Incoming Vancouver, Toronto bumped Dallas back 2 spots
1996	6	6	To Boston with '97 top pick for Celts' top pick (9), Eric Montross
1997	6	6	Pick went to Boston; received pick 15 from Minnesota in '94 trade
1998	6	6	
1999	8	9	Traded to Phoenix in 1998 in deal for Steve Nash

BUCKNER KOed BY OWN IRON FIST

At Buckner's introductory news conference, he described himself as "not somebody who's going to be patient."

"There is a task at hand and we've got to approach it with a sense of urgency," Buckner said. "We can't afford to be complacent."

That wasn't just telling the fans what they wanted to hear. He really expected to win now, even if he didn't have players to do it. That was his first mistake. The next one was insisting on using the Triangle offense, a complex system that takes years to install and had only been successful with Michael Jordan running it.

It's admirable that Buckner thought so highly of himself, his team and his scheme. But his stubbornness set him up to fail, further hindering a team that couldn't afford to keep throwing away seasons.

A big part of the problem was the way Buckner treated people. Apparently, he learned more from the Bob Knight School of Alienation than from the warm embrace of broadcasting or in being from a family full of teachers. When Buckner was rude to reporters at an annual preseason gabfest, it was seen as a stunt to let everyone know the new boss meant business. But it wasn't a stunt. Buckner acted that way within the organization, feuding with everyone from top players to low-rung gofers.

Harper could've been Buckner's locker-room ally, but instead he was one of the first to turn against him. Harper escaped in January, getting traded to the Knicks, reuniting him with Blackman.

Buckner figured his five-year contract bought him time, and his chummy relationship with Sund gave him freedom. Buckner knew that Sund needed him to be a success to keep his own job, which gave the coach the upper hand in their dealings. (For example, Buckner brought in former Portland general manager Stu Inman as a consultant, which many considered a slap to Sund.)

Once Mashburn and Jackson rebelled, Carter told Buckner he needed some help. He soon turned to an outsider—a retiree named Motta.

FAREWELL, RICK ... AND YOUR COACH, TOO

The boy wonder was a man now. Rick Sund, the first employee hired by general manager Norm Sonju, had been with the team through its 14-season rise and fall. Hired at 28 as player personnel director, he was now vice president of basketball operations. It was his job to make the Mavericks rise again. And it wasn't happening.

So Carter did something he hoped to never do: He fired Sund. Carter once said Sund would be in his will as long as he owned the team. But the team had never been so badly in need of a change, and Carter realized it would take some tough decisions to get it started.

Buckner was next, fired 10 days after the season ended. Carter said the coach burned bridges from start to finish.

"You can find lots of places where we should have smelled the wood burning," Carter said.

13

Motta Returns, Kidd Arrives

BACK TO THE PAST

The first thing to remember about Dick Motta's abrupt, bewildering retirement is that Donald Carter never wanted it to happen. Carter never held a grudge and even called him often for advice. They also met for breakfast whenever Motta was in town. Carter made no secret that he wanted back the man he always called "Coach." But his wife and family wouldn't hear of it. Their feelings were still hurt over the way Motta left.

Motta returned to coaching in Sacramento, had two awful years, then was fired on Christmas Eve 1991. He was so sure his sideline days were done that he began collecting Social Security. Then Quinn Buckner drew Motta back into the fold—with Carter's urging. Motta insisted he was just looking around and offering advice.

When Carter fired Buckner, he asked Motta to come up with a list of replacements. Motta put himself at the top. Both, however, knew they needed the blessing of Carter's wife, Linda.

Motta broke the ice months earlier on the maiden voyage of the team's new plane by having a stewardess serve her a plate of oysters. It wasn't a peace offering as much as a good-natured jab in the ribs, the kind friends share. Linda knew the source of the slimy dish and turned to Motta, prompting a pleasant conversation.

The inside joke dates to the 1984 playoffs, when Linda told Motta she would eat raw oysters if the Mavericks beat Seattle in Game 4. They did, and on the flight home for the game that would become Moody Madness, she paid her debt. She later called that meal one of her best memories of the team's first 10 seasons.

When it came time to pick a coach, Motta went to the Carters' home and spoke to Linda alone. He said he couldn't take the job if she was still angry about the way he left. Her response said she wasn't, and the path was clear for his return.

THE DICK MOTTA ERA, TAKE TWO

At age 62, Motta was rehired three days shy of the seven-year anniversary of his departure. He said he came back to fix all that had gone wrong since he left.

"There aren't many people who get a second chance to do something they probably should have done better the first time," Motta said. "I'm really jacked up. I'm going to take every precaution to make sure the team progresses.

"There's no greater thrill than seeing a player develop the way Derek Harper, Rolando Blackman, Mark Aguirre and those guys did. Now I want to make sure Jim Jackson, Jamal Mashburn and these young players develop nicely."

Motta also planned to groom Brad Davis as his replacement.

FROM WASHING SOCKS
TO CALLING THE SHOTS

The day Motta was hired, the Mavericks also named Keith Grant director of player personnel, capping one of the great rises in all of pro sports.

Grant joined the Mavericks on Labor Day weekend in 1980. He was 22 and fresh out of Oklahoma City University. Although he had a degree in business management, the Mavericks hired him to be their first equipment manager.

Grant had worked for Oklahoma City's minor-league baseball team since 1970, starting as a batboy. Other roles he held through the years included shining shoes and washing uniforms.

His first break in Dallas came in 1981 for the simple reason that his apartment had cable television. The team gave him a VCR and had him tape as many games as possible. He'd pass on the tapes to assistant coach Bob Weiss, then watched as Weiss studied them. Grant was soon breaking down tapes on his own and eventually began putting together clips of potential draft choices. He became so good at analyzing players that he was sent to scout NBA games and small colleges.

Grant moved up to administrative assistant/scout for two years, then to pro scout from 1986-87. He even got to coach in a summer rookie league and did some number crunching to help Sonju with contracts. He was named director of scouting in 1990.

Grant's opinion became respected within the organization—especially after his advice was ignored and later proved to have been right. One example was in 1989, when he pushed for Tim Hardaway to be drafted over Randy White. He also became respected within the league for helping run the Chicago pre-draft camp.

His role in Dallas was reduced when Buckner arrived, then ramped up again when Sund was fired. Carter made Grant his go-to guy, even having him work with Motta to identify candidates to become the next coach.

Now his task was to prepare for his first draft.

1994 DRAFT:
THE JASON KIDD-GRANT HILL DEBATE

The Mavericks came out of the lottery with the second pick, which was fine because Milwaukee was expected to take Glenn Robinson first. That left Dallas the choice of either Jason Kidd or Grant Hill. Within the organization, it was an easy call.

Motta repeatedly said that when he came into the league in the 1960s there were five great centers and five great point guards. He believed that was still the case today and that Kidd would instantly be one of those elite floor leaders. Best of all, he'd be plugged into a lineup that already had prototypes at shooting guard (Jackson) and small forward (Mashburn). The possibilities were mouth-watering. The marketing department especially loved the idea of "Three Js." Hill's representatives were so convinced that Dallas was taking Kidd that they refused to visit.

The Mavericks indeed took Kidd; then Grant and Motta went back to work. They also had the 19th and 28th picks, giving this draft the potential to be a blockbuster like 1981, when Dallas got Mark Aguirre, Rolando Blackman and Jay Vincent. But remember what era of the Mavericks we're talking about.

Dallas took Tony Dumas—who never lived up to expectations—at No. 19, instead of Wesley Person. Deon Thomas was the team's other pick, and he never made the club.

THE GREAT MIRAGE: 1994-95

Hope was a word used often in 1994-95. Tease might have been more appropriate, because that's what this team ended up being. It's fitting, too, because this was the year Roy Tarpley returned.

Kidd signed a $54.23 million, nine-year contract a month before training camp opened, then came within a rebound of a triple-double in his debut. By the 10th game of the season, Mashburn had broken the club record with 50 points—and Jackson had matched it. They were only the sixth pair of teammates to hit 50 in the same season; others in that group included Wilt Chamberlain, George Gervin, Larry Bird and Jerry West.

Buses rolled through Dallas with pictures of the Three Js smiling and laughing, with Mashburn spinning a ball on one finger. The trio did ads wearing leather cowboy hats, chaps and spurs over their uniforms, using a Western theme to welcome "the new Kidd in town."

Motta was named Coach of the Month for November, and Mashburn earned Player of the Week in early December. A victory on December 30 made Dallas 13-12, matching the previous season's win total and marking the latest in a season that the Mavs had been over .500 since 1989-90.

However, an eight-game losing streak in January ruined any chance of making the playoffs. Then on February 24, Jackson suffered a severe ankle sprain that would eventually derail his career. At the time, he was fifth in the league in scoring, and Mashburn was sixth.

With Jackson out, Kidd asserted himself more. He was named Player of the Week in mid-March, then Rookie of the Month. On April 5, he notched his first triple-double. His timing was perfect as it came on "Jason's 'In Your Face'" night, with everyone at Reunion Arena getting cardboard cutouts of his face on a popsicle stick. Thousands of

Handed out to fans at Reunion Arena as a promotional gift on what ended up being the night of Jason Kidd's first career triple-double, these "masks" provided big laughs on The Tonight Show.

Kidd faces were waved every time he made a great play, and there were lots of them.

The Mavericks finished the season with 36 wins, an amazing 23 more than the previous season. Dallas also was only one game under .500 (27-28) when Tarpley played.

The team put together a highlight video promoting Kidd for Rookie of the Year, called "Would We Kidd You?" The cover included gushing quotes and a cartoon of No. 5 throwing a behind-the-back pass.

The video did its job. Kidd received the most prestigious honor ever won by a Maverick—the Rookie of the Year Award. Actually, he shared it with Grant Hill, but as Carter noted, the trophy doesn't have "Co-" on it.

"As long as it says, 'Jason Kidd, Rookie of the Year,' nobody can take that away from me," Kidd said.

Between his play and his smile, Kidd quickly established himself as a fan favorite throughout the NBA, a status cemented on Memorial Day when he appeared on the *Tonight Show with Jay Leno*—and when Leno and the entire studio audience held up the cutouts of Kidd's face.

"You came here and you were Jason Kidd," Carter said. "You're still Jason Kidd, but now you're 'Jason the man.'"

DALLAS 156, HOUSTON 147

Rockets coach Rudy Tomjanovich called it "by far the most bizarre game I've ever been involved with." Motta was so amazed that he kept the box score, something he'd done only twice before in his long career.

"I don't think there's ever been a game like that in the history of the NBA," he said.

Houston was the reigning NBA champion, but was playing without ailing superstar Hakeem Olajuwon.

That was nothing compared to Dallas's woes. Jackson had been out for weeks, and his replacement, Lucious Harris, was out, too. Kidd's neck was so sore that he considered not playing because he could hardly turn left before tipoff. He also could've used the rest because it was the Mavericks' second game in two nights, fourth in five and fifth in seven.

The Mavs trailed by 12 to start the fourth quarter, but scored on 17 of their last 18 possessions to go up by eight with 52.9 seconds left. Then Houston started fouling, and Dallas responded by making eight free throws. Yet it wasn't enough. The Rockets rallied with 16 points of their own, including four three-pointers. Sam Cassell hit the last one while off balance in the left corner with 1.9 seconds remaining. That tied it at 119, forcing overtime. There had been 24 points scored in the last 52.9 seconds!

Although it was April 11, Houston hadn't been to overtime all season. The Mavericks had gone six times and won four, all on the road against playoff-bound teams.

In OT, Houston led by 11 with a minute to go. Then came Dallas's incredible spurt. The Mavs were within five points when Kidd stole a pass in the backcourt and hit a three-pointer while falling out of bounds with 22.3 seconds left.

Moments later, the Rockets led by three when Kidd caught an inbounds pass, raced to the three-point line and jumped to get away from Mario Elie. Kidd's leaning, double-clutching shot swished with 2.5 seconds left, forcing another overtime. It was Kidd's eighth three-pointer of the game—a team record—and his sixth in a row.

"After Jason hit that ... it was like we fooled ourselves into having fresh legs," said Popeye Jones, who had 21 rebounds. "That was incredible."

Jamal Mashburn scored seven of his 42 points in the second OT, including a three-point play that put Dallas up by four with 1:21 left.

The Rockets were out of answers. Kidd scored the game's final five points, somehow having the energy to soar for a dunk with 13.5 seconds left to seal the 156-147 victory.

"I kept waiting for the game to come to me," joked Kidd, who scored a season-high 38 points to go with 11 rebounds and

10 assists. "And we were out there so long that I guess it finally did."

It was the most points the Mavericks had ever scored, as well as the most they'd allowed. They also made a team-best 28 three-pointers.

"It was the kind of game you can't wait to tell your grandkids about," Kidd said. "I don't think anybody who played in it, watched it or even sold popcorn at it will ever forget it."

Many of the fans who were there for the start missed the fabulous finishes.

"There were two types of people who left the game early," assistant coach Brad Davis said. "The type who thought we won in regulation and the type who thought the Rockets won in overtime."

COMIC RELIEF

Forget the thumbs-up, thumbs-down movie review system. For Mavericks fans in 1994-95, the best film advice came from Popeye Jones and Tony Dumas.

Continuing the popular "Players on Film" segment begun the previous season by Jones and Tim Legler, the pair cracked everyone up with reviews shown on Reunion's big screen.

Favorites got four hoops. Stinkers got none. The best part was their commentary, which even distracted Motta. The coach once spent a whole timeout watching and laughing.

Dumas gave fans more to laugh about that season by going 0 for three at the dunk contest.

14

The Three Js

BACK IN THE WRONG DIRECTION

The 1995-96 season began with promise: a franchise-best 4-0 start. Then came seven straight losses and a litany of problems. Dallas didn't win more than two straight the rest of the season. They had no problem losing in bunches, such as an 11-game skid in March.

Between Thanksgiving and Christmas, Roy Tarpley was banned again, Jamal Mashburn suffered a season-ending knee injury, and Dick Motta's father died, sapping the coach's desire and focus. By spring, Motta rarely held practices. He turned the last 27 games into a glorified shooting exhibition, and the Mavericks shattered league records for three-pointers made (735) and attempted (2,309). No team since has made 700 or tried 2,000.

THE THREE Js (Juvenile, Jealous, Jabbering)

Personality clashes were inevitable with the Three Js.

Think about it: Each came in as high draft picks, All-Americans who were among the best players in their school's history. They'd always been *the* star on teams and were now filthy rich.

But the Mavericks wanted them to be a unit, which meant sharing the spotlight. Had Derek Harper or Rolando Blackman still been around, maybe they could have told the youngsters to straighten up. Instead, the Mavericks were the league's youngest team with an average age of under 26.

The danger signs were everywhere, and Motta knew it. Asked once if Popeye Jones was becoming "the fourth J," Motta responded that "jealousy" was.

Mashburn and Jackson clashed first. They stopped talking early in the season. Motta demanded they work it out, while teammates blamed both for playing selfishly.

Kidd held his tongue until February. After setting a team-record with 25 assists in a double-overtime victory against Utah, then becoming the first Maverick to start the All-Star game, Kidd said he lost respect for the other Js because of their feud. He then suggested that he should be the team's leader. At least, that's what he meant when he said, "Why shouldn't I just go buy my own boat and have everybody jump on my boat, instead of everybody getting in their boat, when we don't know who's steering the boat?"

Kidd and Jackson stopped talking. Next, Kidd declared that he didn't think the team was big enough for both of them. Then *The Dallas Morning News* reported that part of their problem was a fight over a woman, later identified as Toni Braxton. According to the most-told version of events, Kidd was supposed to meet the sultry rhythm and blues singer outside the team hotel while in Atlanta for a game on December 1, 1995, but Jackson got into her limousine instead.

Both players still adamantly reject that tale. Braxton had a chance to extinguish the rumor, but instead kept it alive through a coy "no comment" in an interview with *The Morning News* in June 1996.

The three Js combination of small forward Jamal Mashburn (left), point guard Jason Kidd (center), and shooting guard Jim Jackson was perfect on paper. But the reality played out more like an Old West shootout. (NBAE/Getty Images)

"I can never kiss and tell," she said.

It's worth mentioning that Braxton was trying to promote an album—one that happened to be titled *Secrets.* So being linked to this quarrel kept her name in the news, and you know the saying about the only bad publicity being none at all.

While Kidd emerged from the mess with only a smudged reputation, Jackson's career was never the same. In 2002-03, his 11th season, he played for his ninth team.

MR. C SELLS

On May 1, 1996, Donald Carter celebrated the 16th anniversary of the day the Dallas basketball team was unveiled by giving up his title of majority owner. The team that cost $12 million to start was sold for $125 million to a group of investors led by real estate mogul Ross Perot Jr. and auto dealer David McDavid. At a news conference, it also was announced that Motta was moving from coach to consultant.

"Coach Motta and I talked about this a long time, about when this day came whether we might have a couple of horses up here and ride off into the sunset together," Carter said.

For years, McDavid had been asking his friend Carter when he was going to sell him the team. Once Carter said he was ready, McDavid got Perot to join him—and to take more than 51 percent.

"The people that know me are very surprised I'm up here right now," said Perot, whose knowledge of basketball was limited at best.

Perot said McDavid would "run the team day in and day out." The team also announced that Norm Sonju would remain as president/general manager.

The front office, however, was soon remade again. Sonju was forced into retirement a few weeks later when the search for Motta's replacement went awry, costing them a chance at Indiana's oft-traveled coach Larry Brown. McDavid gave way to minority owner Frank Zaccanelli, president of Perot's Hillwood Development Corp. He took charge of the search for a coach and a GM.

Keith Grant, the last link to the previous regime, was told he wasn't a candidate to become GM, but he agreed to handle those duties until a replacement could be found. He remained the de facto GM until resigning in October.

Carter retained a minority stake, as did his three remaining original partners—Horace Ardinger, Hal Browning and Lindsey Embrey.

"My wife and I have had the responsibility and the pressure," Carter said. "We'll start being more like grandparents. We'd like to think we've been pretty good owners, and I'd like to think we'll be even better grandparents."

15

Anyone Can Have a Bad Decade, Right?

THE HIRING OF JIM CLEAMONS

Jim Cleamons could've been an original Maverick. He was taken from Washington in the dispersal draft, and two months later, his coach with the Bullets, Dick Motta, was hired in Dallas. He retired instead. Given a second chance to join the franchise as its coach, he gladly accepted.

Cleamons was hired May 31, 1996. Among his selling points was a connection to the two winningest teams in NBA history. He played on the 1971-72 Lakers team that went 69-13 and was an assistant coach with the 1995-96 Bulls team that upped the record to 72-10.

His plan to turn things around in Dallas was to get everyone—including Jason Kidd and Jim Jackson—to buy into a team concept. Or else.

"Discipline is the cornerstone of my life, and that's what I think life is all about," Cleamons said at his introductory news conference. "At times, I put my arm around players and then at times I get the whip out. You can't have a team without harmony."

Cleamons returned to the Bulls for a few weeks to help them win a fourth championship, then arrived in Dallas just in time for the draft—and another round of Kidd vs. Jackson. His fifth day on the job was spent defusing a story in the *Fort Worth Star-Telegram* in which Kidd demanded either he or Jackson be traded. He also said he'd sit out the next season if it didn't happen.

"I understand everything isn't great, but the fact remains: On what basketball club or what work environment is everything great? You can find ways to work around situations and put your best foot forward," Cleamons said.

Minority owner Frank Zaccanelli oversaw the hiring of Cleamons, and the two quickly became a decision-making tandem, with input from Grant, until he left in October, and Mark Aguirre, who'd been friends with Zaccanelli for many years. Aguirre's formal title was scout and director of player development.

MAVS MAN

Cleamons wasn't the only heralded arrival for the 1996-97 season. There also was a high-flying mascot named Mavs Man who quickly became a bigger attraction than the team.

Wearing a basketball-like bodysuit that made him look like a rubberized cousin of Spider-Man, Mavs Man was created after the new owners decided to spruce up the entertainment at home games. He was so popular that he became the focus of marketing campaigns, which was a credit to him and a sad reflection on the players.

Then again, Mavs Man had a better year than they did. Once his original mask was altered to reduce a scary-looking jutting chin, he interacted great with kids and adults. Everyone marveled at his acrobatic dunks. The Utah Jazz were so impressed that they invited him to their place for the NBA Finals. A few months later, he performed in Paris. Then London.

His true identity was fiercely protected. A rumor spread that it was Jimmy King, a former high school star in suburban Plano who'd been part of Michigan's Fab Five squad. King had tried out for the Mavericks, but didn't make it.

Or did he?

THUD! CLEAMONS NOT THE ANSWER EITHER

Try not to roll your eyes if you've heard this before: With a roster filled with exciting newcomers and a promising new coach, the Mavericks went into the season believing they were bound to be better, if for no reason other than they couldn't get much worse. And yet, they still did. After winning the '96-97 opener, Dallas lost four straight. The Mavs finished November at 4-10, and infighting again was a dominant theme.

Jamal Mashburn came back so slowly from a knee injury that he was backing up George McCloud. He also missed eight early games because of a broken cheekbone. That couldn't stop him from spouting off about his role and hinting he wouldn't mind being traded.

Derek Harper was re-signed in hopes that he'd provide the veteran voice that was missing. But he found players not willing to listen. They were too concerned about stats, endorsements and other things they valued more than wins and losses. A blatant example came when Tony Dumas laughed and slapped hands with Mashburn after airballing a free throw during a 30-point loss.

There also were plenty of complaints about Cleamons, mostly involving the Triangle offense he insisted on installing. That cerebral, restrictive system was the exact opposite of the jack-it-up approach Motta had used. Plus, the Triangle offense already had failed once in Dallas under Buckner.

The only bright spot was free agent signee Chris Gatling. He led the team in scoring and rebounding despite coming off the bench and made the All-Star team, an impressive feat for a backup on one of the league's worst teams.

GETTING TAKEN FOR A RIDE

A decade after the scary flight on Charlie Pride's plane, Aguirre and Harper went on another long, strange trip.

It was November 1996, and the Mavs were flying home from Detroit. Bad weather forced the team plane to land in Austin. They arrived about the same time as the storm.

The landing was so rough that Harper and McCloud threw up.

"Harp was stiff as a board, asking me if everything was going to be all right," Dumas said.

Dumas, Harper and McCloud refused to fly home. So they piled into one cab, and Aguirre and Zaccanelli took another—all the way to Dallas. Each fare was $225. They arrived around 7 a.m., about three hours after those who took the plane.

TRADING JASON KIDD

Kidd and Cleamons had little common ground. Cleamons wanted a slow, methodical approach. Kidd wanted to speed it up. Cleamons was the boss. Kidd thought it was his team. Cleamons got Michael Jordan to tell Kidd to give the coach a chance. Kidd didn't.

Kidd lost his teammates' respect by skipping practices and not working on his shot, which certainly needed polishing. His accuracy had dropped from 38.5 percent as a rookie to 38.1 and finally 36.9 percent.

Fans who loved his razzle-dazzle dribbling and passing were tiring of his off-court antics. Cleamons and Zaccanelli finally decided enough was enough. After 22 tension-filled games, they stunned the basketball world by trading Kidd to Phoenix on December 26, 1996, along with Dumas and Loren Meyer. In return, Dallas received youngster Michael Finley, veteran A.C. Green and Sam Cassell, who would take over for Kidd immediately but was a free agent after the season.

"We understand the magnitude of what we've just done," Zaccanelli said that night. "We think we've taken a step in the right direction."

When people said Zaccanelli had traded away "a franchise player," he agreed.

"That was part of the problem," he said. "No one player makes a franchise."

Whether he meant to bash Kidd or hype Cassell, Cleamons said the swap of point guards was "a wash, tit for tat." It was a laughable statement. Cassell had helped Houston win two NBA titles, but he'd never been a full-time starter. Kidd already had been co-Rookie of the Year and an All-Star starter.

To describe the motivation behind the deal in one word, it would be "character." The Mavericks felt Kidd didn't have enough of it. Finley, Cassell and Green all had solid reputations. Talent, though, is what wins basketball games, which is why the deal was widely blasted. If Cleamons and Zaccanelli were so determined to trade Kidd, they probably could've shopped for a better deal.

Cleamons was still trying to spin the deal when the newcomers arrived for an introductory news conference. When they described themselves as team players who put winning ahead of individual accolades, Cleamons smiled, nodded and blurted, "Somebody say amen!"

"I was asking for one guy to step up to the table and buy into what I'm trying to do," Cleamons said. "Now, lo and behold, I get three guys. I'm happy!"

Kidd was pleased, too.

"I never thought they would trade me," he said after arriving in Phoenix. "But I am really excited about this opportunity. Mentally, I feel great, like I am a new person. Everyone will see the old Jason playing."

SCRAPPED

The Three Js experiment was over—and it was a failure. Of a possible 189 games together, all three played in just 80. Dallas went 29-51 in those games, for a .363 winning percentage. The Mavs were 42-67 with only one or two, a .385 winning clip.

After dealing Kidd, they looked to get rid of the other two Js. They nearly sent Jackson and Eric Montross to the Clippers for guard Brent Barry and holdout forward Brian Williams, but Dallas doctors didn't like Williams's knee. Another deal that fell apart would've sent Mashburn to the Pacers for forwards Derrick McKey and Duane Ferrell and a first-round pick. Indiana wanted to make it Mashburn for McKey.

THE IRONMAN

A.C. Green was playing only his 67th game for Dallas when he hit number 907 in a row for his career, breaking the league's longevity record. Sure, it was a great feat. But it wasn't exactly part of Mavericks lore, which is why the team's overblown celebration is grouped with this depressing era.

During a 23-minute halftime celebration, the team raised a banner emblazoned with "907." Green became only the second player to receive such permanent, personal glory. Green also received a rocking chair, a $10,000 donation to the A.C. Green Youth Foundation and a snazzy leather jacket with the word "Ironman" emblazoned on a sleeve. The date—November 20, 1997—was etched on the back collar.

What he didn't get was a victory. Dallas lost 101-97 to an 0-9 Warriors team, the worst start in that franchise's history.

CLEAMONS CANNED

When Cleamons was fired on December 4, 1997, the Mavericks had dropped 12 of 13. In his final three weeks, they lost by 45, 33 and 21 in a game when they scored a franchise-low 62 points.

"We basically saw our franchise heading in the wrong direction," said general manager Don Nelson, who replaced Cleamons as coach.

Fan support was dwindling, too, and the team couldn't afford that—not six weeks before a vote on a new arena.

Cleamons left with a 28-70 record and one claim to fame: In October 1996, he guided the Mavericks to their first team trophy, even if all it took was winning two games in a preseason tournament in Mexico City.

A MISERABLE DECADE

Of all the teams that existed in the four major pro sports on January 1, 1990, the Mavericks had the most miserable decade.

The franchise had seven coaches, three owners, one playoff appearance—and no postseason victories. Dallas lost 310 more games than it played. The Mavericks would've had to go undefeated for nearly four more seasons just to hit .500. There were losing streaks of 20, 19, 17, 16, 15 (three times), 12, 11 (three time) and 10 games.

In the nine full seasons (1990-91 to 1998-99), the Mavs were a total of 328 games out of first place. They never finished higher than fourth in the division or 10th in the conference.

Date	Record	Games Behind	Best Win Streak	Worst Lose Streak
Jan. 1 to April 22, 1990	32-22	4	7	5
1990-91	28-54	27	4	8
1991-92	22-60	33	3	15
1992-93	11-71	44	2	19
1993-94	13-69	45	2	20
1994-95	36-46	26	6	8
1995-96	26-56	33	4-x	11
1996-97	24-58	40	3	11
1997-98	20-62	42	3-x	15
1998-99	19-31	18	4	7
Nov. 2 to Dec. 31, 1999	9-21	16	2	4
Totals:	240-550 (.304)	328		

-x: Came at the start of the season.

SECTION III:

The New Glory Days

(FEBRUARY 7, 1997 TO PRESENT)

16

Mavs Get Their Man: Nelson

THE REVIVAL BEGINS

The Dallas Mavericks were a muddled mess, and the new owners knew it.

It was early 1997, eight months after a group led by Ross Perot Jr. bought the team from founder Don Carter. President and general manager Norm Sonju retired two weeks after the ownership change, and the team was being run by minority owner Frank Zaccanelli—the head of Perot's real-estate development company—and the coach he'd hired, Jim Cleamons.

Cleamons came from the Chicago Bulls and insisted on using their Triangle offense. It was a huge failure and was straining relations with players, especially his best one, Jason Kidd.

So Kidd was traded in a deal that got Dallas ridiculed, convincing the new owners that they needed a proven basketball man to take over—pronto. They wanted someone with a successful track record. Someone with instant credibility. Someone whose mere presence would demand respect. And someone who could take over right away.

Someone like Don Nelson. Nelson was living in Maui, his bank account padded—but his reputation damaged—by a brief tenure with the Knicks. Considering he'd also left his previous job under a black cloud, Nelson wanted another chance. So on February 7, 1997, he became just the second general manager of the Dallas Mavericks.

"I never dreamed a month ago I'd be here or be back in the league," Nelson said. "This is quite a challenge, but I'm up to it.

"There's nothing more rewarding than to take a team that's down and build it into a contender. I have done it twice before and I can do it again."

Although Nelson had been named one of the top 10 coaches in league history, he insisted that he had "no plans in my future to coach.

"I'm putting coaching out of my mind to concentrate on being the general manager solely and helping Jimmy all I can," Nelson said. "The buck stops with me."

It didn't take long for him to prove it. While leaving his introductory news conference, Nelson cut overweight, unhappy and unproductive center Oliver Miller, who a week earlier had said, "I don't care any more."

"I don't want people like that around," Nelson said.

Someone Nelson did want around was Keith Grant.

At Nelson's urging, Grant—who had resigned four months earlier, hours before Miller was signed—returned as a consultant. The following year he moved up to director of player personnel, then assistant general manager.

In ditching Miller and bringing back Grant, Nelson was righting two wrongs. It was a clear indication that things were about to turn around for the better.

NO MORE Js

Within 10 days, Nelson remade the team so drastically that all 20 people in the previous season's team picture were gone from the organization. Samaki Walker was the longest-tenured player—and he was drafted in June.

"I haven't seen a team made over in this short of time," Nelson said. "But there were just so many negative things about this ball club."

A key to the makeover was getting rid of Jamal Mashburn and Jim Jackson, who along with Kidd had been heralded as the "Three Js." It was the latest in a decade of failed rebuilding attempts, and now Nelson was beginning another one.

Mashburn was sent to Miami for Dallas native Kurt Thomas (who had a broken ankle at the time), Sasha Danilovic and Martin Muursepp. Jackson went to New Jersey in a nine-player deal, the largest in NBA history. In that swap, Dallas gave up its four leading scorers (Jackson, Chris Gatling, George McCloud and Sam Cassell) and Eric Montross. In return, Shawn Bradley, Robert Pack, Khalid Reeves and Ed O'Bannon became Mavs.

"CORNERSTONES"

Nelson declared that Bradley and Pack "were the cornerstones of the trade" with New Jersey. The label would haunt both players.

Pack was one of the league's fastest players, but was also among the least durable. Bradley was a great shot blocker, but he wasn't much of a scorer or rebounder. And he had a huge contract.

By the time the Mavericks reached the playoffs in 2001, Bradley was a starter but not a key player, and Pack was long gone. He played only 86 games for Dallas over parts of four seasons.

To best understand how far both players plummeted, consider their roles in a 2002 first-round playoff series between the Mavericks and Minnesota Timberwolves. Bradley played a total of 10 minutes in two games. For Minnesota, Pack also played 10 minutes, spread over three games. He had no assists and more fouls (five) than points (three).

Bradley did make one significant contribution to team history. He became the first Maverick to lead the league in a statistical category by winning the shot-blocking title in 1996-97.

ONE CORNERSTONE ALREADY IN PLACE

Nelson didn't completely turn over the roster he inherited. One player outlasted the purge: Michael Finley.

Finley came into the league with Phoenix as the 21st pick in the 1995 draft, nine picks after Dallas took Cherokee Parks. He immediately proved he should've gone in the lottery.

Finley played every game as a rookie, starting all but 10, and averaged 15 points. He finished second in the slam dunk contest and third in Rookie of the Year voting and made the All-Rookie team. The only disappointment was that a sprained ankle in the final quarter of the season finale kept him from playing in the playoffs.

The following season his scoring was down a bit around the time the Suns and Mavs started talking trade. Phoenix officials were reluctant to part with him—until he became the final holdup in getting Kidd.

"Michael Finley became the deal maker once his name was added," Cleamons said. "I wasn't going to part with anyone in our organization until Michael Finley was part of the deal."

STILL SOME BOTTOMING OUT TO BE DONE

The Mavericks bottomed out so many times in the 1990s that it was almost like a dribbling basketball. Thump, thump, thump. Just when fans thought Dallas was on the way up, the team was on the way back down again.

The '96-97 season was the final bounce. All the wheeling and dealing produced 18 starters and 27 players. There were three more players than wins! The Mavericks set a franchise low for points in a game with 66 in January. They then scored 65 in March. No wonder the season average was 90 points, their worst ever.

The ultimate embarrassment came April 6 against the Los Angeles Lakers, when Dallas went the entire third quarter with-

*Shawn Bradley didn't turn out to be the "cornerstone" Don Nelson
expected, but with 3.4 blocks per game in 1996-97 he became the first
Maverick to lead the NBA in a statistical category.
(NBAE/Getty Images)*

out a basket. The only points came on a pair of free throws by Derek Harper. The Mavs missed all 15 shots that period—four by Finley, three by Harper, and two each by A.C. Green and Bradley. The previous lowest-scoring quarter by an NBA team was four. Sadly, Dallas had been leading 51-37 at the start of the third; the Lakers ended the quarter ahead 64-53 and sent the Mavericks to their 11th straight loss.

"I've never seen an exhibition of basketball like that in all my years in this league," Cleamons said.

NELLIE TAKES OVER—COMPLETELY

Don Nelson had finally seen enough. On December 4, 1997, the general manager fired Cleamons and gave the job to himself.

Nelson first asked owner Ross Perot Jr. if he could dump Cleamons in April, but was told to wait. Perot gave in this time after a 4-12 start.

Nellie-ball was a radical change from Cleamons's ineffective, plodding system. He went with a smaller lineup and told them to have fun. Dallas won his debut 105-91 over the Knicks, the team that had fired Nelson 21 months before.

"I don't think there was anybody better qualified outside to hire to bring into this tough situation than me," Nelson said. "Not that we're going to win championships yet, but I believe we can play better basketball than we've been playing and have more fun doing it."

Nelson was as qualified as anyone to run the Mavericks on the court and in the front office. He played in the league 14 seasons, winning five championships with the Boston Celtics and getting his No. 19 retired.

He went straight into coaching, starting as an assistant in Milwaukee then getting promoted after just 18 games. Nelson lasted 11 seasons, winning seven straight division titles and being voted Coach of the Year twice. Yet he never won an NBA title or even made the finals. Great Boston and Philadelphia teams always got in the way.

Nelson put together the Bucks' winning roster through trades and drafts. Dallas's original personnel director, Rick Sund, even got his start in the NBA working for Nelson. Nelson's ties to Sund and Norm Sonju, the Mavericks' first GM, almost landed him in Dallas after he left Milwaukee in the summer of '87. Instead, he wound up going to the Golden State Warriors.

In Oakland, Nelson continued his dual-role success. He had two 50-win seasons and was named Coach of the Year a third time. His playoff woes continued, too, as he won just two series in seven seasons. He was fired during the '94-95 season following a bitter dispute with Chris Webber. He tried rebounding the next season with the Knicks, but a plan to ease the load on Patrick Ewing led to his demise.

Although the Mavericks finished his first season with four more losses than the previous year, things were looking up. Dallas went 8-8 in March, making it the most successful month in three years. It included a thrilling overtime victory against Michael Jordan and the Bulls.

THE MAD SCIENTIST

Conventional is not a word used to describe Nelson's coaching style. He proved that in his first few months with the Mavericks.

In his fifth game, Nelson tried ending a 15-game losing streak in Utah by running down the shot clock on every possession. It sort of worked, as Dallas had a chance to win at the buzzer, but Dennis Scott failed to take an open three-pointer and the Mavericks lost 68-66.

Against Chicago a few weeks later, Nelson decided to foul Dennis Rodman any time he could go to the free throw line. Seldom-used rookie Bubba Wells was the hit man and fouled out in just three minutes. The plan backfired as Rodman, a 38.6-percent foul shooter, hit nine of 12 and the Bulls won 111-105.

But Nelson did accomplish one thing: Wells went into the NBA record book for fastest disqualification.

SUCCESSION PLAN

After less than a month as Dallas's coach, Don Nelson hired a successor—his son, Donnie. The catch: He wouldn't take over until 2000-01.

Donnie was a highly regarded assistant in Phoenix. The Suns had even given him a rare five-year contract with a clause that prevented him from leaving unless it was to become a head coach. Although the Mavericks didn't exactly do that, it was close enough. Donnie was named director of scouting and coach-in-waiting ... and it happened while Dallas was playing in Phoenix. His father told reporters before the game, then went on the pregame broadcast and announced it to fans.

"When I get this thing headed in the right direction, he'll take over the reins," said Don Nelson, who by this point was under contract as coach through 2000 and GM through 2003.

"I know I'm biased, but I consider him one of the brightest young coaches in the league, and now he's ours."

Phoenix let him go without any compensation, but there was one provision—he wasn't allowed to help the Mavs prepare for that night's game. He didn't, and Dallas lost, making it 14 straight since winning Nellie's debut.

UNFORGETTA-BULL

On March 12, 1998, the two-time defending champion Chicago Bulls came to Dallas to face a team that was 13-49 and had lost two straight. The Mavericks had played so poorly in their last game that Rockets forward Charles Barkley said, "I don't think they could win the NCAAs."

As expected, Chicago led by 17 with 5:43 to play. A crowd of 18,255, the largest ever for a sporting event at Reunion Arena, began to leave as Michael Jordan seemed done for the night. Everything had to go wrong for Chicago and right for Dallas for the Mavericks to even have a chance.

Amazingly, both happened. The Bulls didn't make a field goal in the final 3:44. They even struggled from the foul line—Steve Kerr, a 94 percent free throw shooter, missed two straight, and Jordan went two of four.

In the last 16.1 seconds, Dallas got a dunk from Cedric Ceballos, a jumper from Hubert Davis and a you-had-to-see-it-to-believe-it three-pointer from Ceballos for the tie. Making Ceballos's last shot even more improbable was the fact the Mavericks got the ball back because Scottie Pippen wasn't able to throw an inbounds pass after Davis's basket.

Chicago still had a chance to win at the buzzer, but Toni Kukoc missed a layup.

Ceballos opened overtime with a dunk. It was the first time the Mavericks led in the game, and they wouldn't trail again.

Jordan had a chance to pull off his usual heroics, but failed. He badly missed a wide-open three-pointer that would've given Chicago the lead. In the final minute, he tried stealing the ball from Finley but missed and fell, setting up an easy basket for Dallas.

Bulls coach Phil Jackson was so disgusted that he headed to the locker room before time expired.

The 104-97 victory was so memorable that the Mavericks sent a tape of the game to season ticket holders instead of an annual highlights film.

17

Dirk and Steve to the Rescue

JUNE 24, 1998

Other than the day the franchise was born, June 24, 1998, is arguably the second most important date in team history. It was the day Dirk Nowitzki and Steve Nash became Mavericks.

It didn't seem monumental at the time. In typical Nelson fashion, it was a big gamble. Nowitzki was a 20-year-old wunderkind from Germany who wasn't even sure he wanted to play in the NBA yet. He talked about spending a year or two in Europe first. Nash was the third-string point guard in Phoenix playing behind Jason Kidd and Kevin Johnson. Although he'd started only 11 games, he was expected to be a hot free agent the following summer.

Here's how both became Mavericks:

With the sixth overall pick, Dallas took Robert Traylor as part of a prearranged deal with Milwaukee. The Bucks then took Nowitzki ninth, one spot ahead of Boston. That rankled Celtics coach Rick Pitino because he had his sights set on the big German. The Bucks also took Pat Garrity at No. 19 and swapped Garrity and Nowitzki for Traylor. The Mavs then packaged

Garrity, Martin Muursepp, Bubba Wells and next year's top pick for Nash.

"Things could not have gone better," Nelson said that night. "Everything we wanted to accomplish, we did. That doesn't happen very much in life."

Fans weren't exactly thinking the same thing.

Mavericks draft history is littered with big white guys taken in the first round who couldn't play a lick—Bill Garnett, Uwe Blab, even Chris Anstey, Nelson's top pick the previous year. The popular choice would've been Paul Pierce, a sharpshooter from Kansas who surprisingly was available at No. 6. He ended up being Pitino's consolation prize at No. 10.

The risk with Nowitzki wasn't just that he might be a bust. There also was the question of when he'd even join the Mavericks. With his mother encouraging him to stay close to home, Nowitzki talked about remaining overseas to improve his game and bulk up his 6-foot-11, 237-pound frame. He was considering offers to play in Italy, Spain or Greece. He'd also thought about going to college at Cal or Kentucky.

Donnie Nelson had worked with Nowitzki for a week in March. His team had stopped in Dallas to practice before going to San Antonio for the Nike Hoop Summit, a tournament held during the NCAA's Final Four. Donnie knew then that Nowitzki was going to be a star—but he didn't want to share his secret. He ran a classic misdirection play out of his father's pre-draft handbook, telling reporters Nowitzki was too soft to make it in the NBA. Nowitzki, who had fled his German club team for this event, almost blew the Mavs' secret by putting up 33 points and 14 rebounds in a game against top U.S. high school players.

"He's 20 years old and loaded with talent," Don Nelson said on draft night. "I don't want you to think we're going to get Larry Bird here in his first year, but he's a very exciting player."

Donnie Nelson also was a key voice in the decision to get Nash. Having worked with him in Phoenix, Nelson was confident Nash could run an NBA offense. His dad believed it, too, saying: "This is going to be Steve's team. We're going to build around him."

DELIVERING DIRK

After drafting Nowitzki, Don Nelson called him and asked for a favor.

"Make sure you don't sign a contract before we talk to you," Nelson said.

The next day, the Nelsons flew to Germany to convince Nowitzki he was ready for the NBA. Team owner Ross Perot Jr. already was doing business in Europe and joined them for the sales pitch.

Nowitzki grew up in Wurzburg, a city of 125,000 residents located about 75 miles southeast of Frankfurt in the center of a wine region. It's one of the northernmost stops along the Romantic Road, a 180-mile stretch of medieval villages that leads to the Bavarian Alps. Every June, Wurzburg hosts a popular Mozart Festival. There are many historic sites, including a 420-year-old university best known for physicist Wilhelm Conrad Roentgen discovering X-rays while teaching there in 1895. Nowitzki's club team was even nicknamed the X-rays.

Nowitzki was a lanky teen still learning basketball basics when Holger Geschwindner first saw him play. Geschwindner, a member of Germany's 1972 Olympic basketball team, saw the boy's potential immediately, and a teacher-student relationship blossomed.

While former Maverick Detlef Schrempf was the greatest German basketball export at the time, Nowitzki didn't grow up idolizing his countryman. The walls of his bedroom featured posters of Michael Jordan, Charles Barkley, and the player Nowitzki most closely modeled his game after: Scottie Pippen.

The Nowitzki family was full of athletes. Dirk's father, Joerg, had been a handball star. His mother, Helga, had played on the national women's basketball team. So did his sister, Silke. She encouraged her brother to become a Maverick, and the Nelsons helped sway Joerg, too. Dirk agreed to fly back to Dallas, accompanied by Geschwindner.

There was little time to waste. Because of a league-wide lockout starting July 1 that would force both sides to stop talking, the team needed a decision. It was already late June.

The final push came with a barbecue at Nelson's home. Nowitzki met some of his prospective teammates and played against Samaki Walker. With Geschwindner telling him to go for it, Nowitzki called home and told his parents he was coming to America.

"They said, 'OK, if you want to do it,'" he said.

Local media had been closely following the Nowitzki saga since the draft, so his decision was announced at a news conference.

"I think my offense is pretty good. I can compete with them," Nowitzki said. "Defense, I have to work hard, learn a bit more. I hope it works out."

FROM B.C. TO THE NBA

Growing up in Victoria, British Columbia, Steve Nash's sports icon was Wayne Gretzky. Outside hockey, his passion was football—well, futbol. His father, John, had been a professional soccer player in South Africa; Steve was even born in Johannesburg, but the family moved to Canada when he was a tot.

Nash began playing basketball when he was 13 mainly because his friends were doing it. He got hooked right away. Patterning his game after Isiah Thomas, Nash started collecting MVP trophies from tournaments.

As a high school sophomore, Nash sprained his left ankle. Forced to jump off his right foot, he began working on his left-handed shot. Anyone who's seen him work his magic around the rim with either hand from any angle now knows how he picked up that skill. (His soccer background explains why he often dribbles loose balls with his feet during breaks in the action.)

His high school coach wrote to about 50 U.S. colleges in hopes of getting Nash a scholarship. The only offer came from

Santa Clara, a Jesuit university with about 9,000 students located at the center of California's Silicon Valley. Interestingly, Santa Clara coach Dick Davey didn't receive one of the letters; one of his assistants had seen Nash on tape.

Nash became a starter halfway through his freshman season. He went on to win West Coast Conference Player of the Year twice while leading the Broncos to two regular-season WCC titles.

He really made his mark in the NCAA tournament. In 1993, he scored six points in the final minute of a first-round upset of Arizona. Nash led the Broncos past Maryland another year.

Up in Oakland, a Golden State assistant heard about the Santa Clara kid, then saw him in summer league games against Tim Hardaway and Jason Kidd. The coach was so impressed that when he went to Phoenix, he convinced the Suns to draft Nash 15th overall even though they already were loaded at point guard. When Nash was buried on the bench, that same coach stuck by him. Then Donnie Nelson went to the Mavericks.

Nash's on-court development will be detailed elsewhere. Here, it's worth mentioning some of his off-court exploits.

He donated $100,000 to help Santa Clara endow a scholarship program, then gave $90,000 to rescue a youth basketball program that was abandoned when the Vancouver Grizzlies left Canada. The Junior Grizzlies, which served more than 8,000 boys and girls ages six to 15, are now called the Steve Nash Youth Basketball Program.

"I felt obligated to do whatever I could to help those kids have an opportunity to play grassroots basketball—something that I never really played," Nash said.

In 2000, while preparing for the Sydney Olympics with Team Canada, Nash wanted his 10 non-NBA teammates to enjoy their stay Down Under. So he had coach Jay Triano give them each $25,000 and asked that the source of the money be kept quiet. The secret came out after the Games.

Nash always considered himself one of the guys on the national team. On one trip, he rode a bus six hours to Montreal and spent the night in a low-budget hotel before making the long ride back. In Sydney, he stayed in the athletes' village. While those gestures might not sound like much, they denote a rare common-man approach for an NBA star.

PUTTING THE "BIG THREE" TOGETHER

Because of a labor dispute that delayed the start of the season, Nowitzki didn't sign until January 21, 1999. Four days later, Nash got a $33 million, six-year contract extension.

At the news conference announcing Nash's deal, Nelson made it clear that he had new cornerstones in Finley, Nash and Nowitzki. Finley and Nash, who were briefly teammates in Phoenix, were even named co-captains.

"The future is in their hands," Nelson said.

Nash moved to Dallas during the lockout and worked out with his soon-to-be teammates. He liked them and the city so much that he was willing to forgo free agency to be tied to a team that hadn't won a playoff game in 11 years.

Nash and Nowitzki also began a friendship that would get stronger every season. Their first homes in Dallas were in the same complex, and they bonded quickly on and off the court, helping each other endure what would be a difficult first season as Mavericks.

EXCITEMENT BREEDS DISAPPOINTMENT

Nelson hyped Nowitzki for Rookie of the Year and built up Nash as the franchise-saving floor leader Jason Kidd was supposed to have been. He also said the team might be able to challenge for the playoffs, a comment that somehow became known as a playoff guarantee.

In retrospect, he was right about it all. He was just a couple years early.

The Mavericks went 19-31 in 1999, their best winning percentage in four years. They closed on an 8-6 roll. But there were plenty of low points, such as all of Nelson's projections going wrong.

"I might have made a mistake on Nowitzki [as a Rookie of the Year candidate]. But it was an honest mistake," Nelson said during the season. "I thought he could score and shoot the ball, but he's struggled there, too. I don't think I oversold Nash, either. He'll be what I said he was. He's too good a player."

NASH'S NIGHT TO FORGET

When Nash missed his eighth shot in a row against Houston on March 24, fans at Reunion Arena began booing. They kept it up nearly every time he touched the ball. Nash opened the second half on the bench, then heard another chorus of boos when he checked in. He grinned slightly, but the rejection clearly affected him. He shot only twice more, including a three-pointer that finally quieted the crowd.

"Way to hang," Nelson told Nash as he headed to the bench for the final 5:35 of an 88-78 loss.

Nash finished one for 10, lowering his season accuracy to 35 percent.

Two games before he'd scored 22 points. And the previous game he had eight assists. So while he wasn't a complete player yet, he certainly had it in him.

"I think in a couple years from now, we'll laugh about how he got booed," Nelson said.

Nash added: "I'll face it with a smile on my face, and I'll be a winner one of these days."

What fans didn't know was that he was trying so hard to please them that he was playing with an injured back.

*Fans were slow to warm to Steve Nash, but once
they did, they even appreciated his mussy hairstyles.
(AP/WWP)*

NOWITZKI'S START

Schrempf, the first German in Mavs history, was on the opposite side when Nowitzki made his Dallas debut. It was an overtime loss in Seattle, and Nowitzki had just two points and no
rebounds in 16 minutes. For the record, his initial points came
on a pair of free throws two minutes into the second half. He was
0 for five from the field.

His confidence was jumpstarted the next game when he got
to cover 5-foot-3 Muggsy Bogues, the shortest player in NBA
history. Nowitzki responded with five rebounds in the first quarter.

Dallas began the season 1-8 with Nowitzki in the starting lineup, so coach Don Nelson moved the rookie to the bench and started veteran Cedric Ceballos.

It wasn't all Nowitzki's fault. Consider the situation he was in. Only 20, he was living in a new country and trying to speak only English for the first time (it wasn't totally new, because he'd studied English in school). He also was going from playing the equivalent of Division II college ball in Germany to the NBA. Plus, the lockout had deprived him of a real training camp.

Nowitzki averaged 8.2 points in 47 games. His defense was so bad that some mockingly referred to him as "Irk," because he had no "D."

He finally broke through late in the season, leading the team in scoring twice during the last 12 games with 29 and 22 points. Most importantly, he didn't wonder whether he would've been better off in Europe.

"I still think it's the right decision," he said. "When I'll be 22 or 23, I think I'll be all right."

18

The Saga of Leon Smith

NO, SAMAKI, NO!

On April 10, 1999, Golden State's Chris Mills nearly became the first opposing player to intentionally score for the Mavericks.

But Samaki Walker didn't let him.

With 9:30 left in a game at Reunion Arena, Mills grabbed a jump ball near the basket the Warriors were shooting at, but took off in the other direction. He tried banking in a layup that would've been two points for Dallas. But Walker chased him down the court and fouled him hard enough to keep the ball from going in.

The Mavericks ended up losing 91-90.

"Luckily," Mills said, "he bailed me out."

NO MORE PREDICTIONS

Don Nelson insisted the 1999-2000 season would be his 22nd and last as a coach. He was looking forward to returning to his

GM-only role and was still planning to let his son, Donnie, take over.

Nelson also knew they both might be gone if the Mavericks didn't start improving. Yet that didn't stop him from making some curious moves. He drafted a Chinese center, traded for a high school player and dumped Chris Anstey, the first first-round pick he made in Dallas, for a second-round selection.

Another change for Nelson was getting out of the prediction business.

"I succumbed to that last year," he said, "and it backfired in my face."

THE SAD STORY OF LEON SMITH

Don and Donnie Nelson had never met Leon Smith or even seen him play. But they liked what they heard from people who had. Smith was a high school phenom from Chicago trying to follow the freshly made footprints of Kevin Garnett and Kobe Bryant by skipping college and going straight to the pros.

Jerry West of the Los Angeles Lakers was rumored to be very high on the kid. The Houston Rockets were thought to be after him, too. Yet it was the Mavericks who made a bold move to get him. Dallas had San Antonio take Smith with the last pick of the first round then send him to the Mavericks. His draft spot was significant because as a first-rounder he was guaranteed a three-year contract worth about $1.45 million.

Unlike last season, when Nelson tried talking Nowitzki out of playing overseas, this time he *wanted* Smith to go to Europe to develop his game.

"If you throw him the ball in the low post, he really doesn't know what to do yet," Nelson said. "But ... you can't teach instinct, and he has that."

Smith, though, hated the idea.

It wasn't just that he wanted to be in the NBA. To him, being shipped away was continuing his rocky childhood, which included being made a ward of the state of Illinois at age five and growing up in five group homes. His anger came lashing out in his first practice. He bickered with Donnie Nelson, threw down his jersey and stormed off. He was kicked out of another practice for not following orders on a defensive drill.

Once Smith began playing in a California summer league, his talent was obvious. With a 6-foot-10 frame, broad shoulders and a wingspan that rivaled 7-foot-6 Shawn Bradley, Smith had 10 points in 12 minutes, 15 points and six rebounds the next time out, then 16 points and 16 rebounds.

Although the Nelsons tried patching their relationship—even canceling practice one day to take him to Disneyland—they still wanted him to develop elsewhere. Smith disagreed. On November 2, his 19th birthday, Smith demanded an NBA deal, which he could do by virtue of being a first-rounder.

"I was always coming to Dallas," he said.

The team put him on the injured list and didn't let him practice with the rest of the team. He left a home game early without talking to anyone.

Then this odd tale nearly turned tragic.

Smith smashed a rock through a friend's windshield and took more than 200 aspirin, prompting a call to police. When officers found him passed out in his apartment with green war paint on his face, he said he "was an Indian and was fighting Columbus." He left behind two suicide notes, one for the Nelsons and another for an ex-girlfriend.

The head of the NBA Players' Association criticized Dallas for not taking better care of the troubled teen. Nelson admitted he might've made a mistake in acquiring Smith, but strongly defended how he'd been handled. Nelson said he and his wife had even offered to adopt Smith.

The blame game was interrupted when Smith went home to Chicago and got into trouble involving guns, vandalism and his ex-girlfriend. The Mavs eventually negotiated a buyout of his contract, and Smith was waived on February 4, 2000.

Smith went from the St. Louis Swarm of the IBL to a failed tryout with the Harlem Globetrotters. He played for the Sioux

Falls (S.D.) Skyforce of the CBA, then was traded to the Gary (Ind.) Steelheads. His play there earned him a contract with the Atlanta Hawks.

On January 15, 2002, Smith dressed for his first official NBA game. Incredibly, it was against the Mavericks. Alas, Smith didn't play. He went to the scorer's table in the closing minutes of the first half, but had trouble getting the snaps off his warmup suit and was left waiting at midcourt. He stayed on the bench the entire second half.

Smith played 14 games for the Hawks, then was traded to Milwaukee but never made their roster.

He resurfaced in the Dallas area in 2003, playing for a week as a member of the Fort Worth Rim Rockers of the United States Basketball League. Smith averaged 18 points and 17 rebounds in three games, then was among seven players who left the team after being told they would be paid less than originally promised.

19

Mark Cuban—
The NBA's New "Maverick"

FROM DOOR-TO-DOOR TO BILLIONAIRE

Growing up in Pittsburgh, Mark Cuban was always angling for a profit. He sold garbage bags door to door. He bought newspapers in Cleveland for a quarter and sold them in Pittsburgh for a buck while the local papers were on strike. After taking college business classes at night while still in high school, he went to Indiana University because it was the cheapest of the 10 best business schools. He ran a bar in Bloomington despite being only 19 years old, too young to own a liquor license.

He wound up in Dallas in 1982, not long after the Mavericks had begun. After selling software, he started MicroSolutions and turned it into one of the nation's leading system integrations firms. CompuServe bought it for $3 million.

Cuban was only 31. The last seven years, he'd worn a suit every day and hadn't taken a vacation or read a book for fun. It was time to reward himself. So he traveled the world and took acting lessons. The biggest role he landed was a bit part in the movie *Talking About Sex;* one of his biggest disappointments was getting rejected for a commercial for a taco chain.

He returned to Dallas in 1994 and soon after created Audionet. What began as a way for Cuban and a friend to listen to radio broadcasts of their beloved Indiana Hoosiers via the internet ended up revolutionizing communications. Thanks to Cuban's creativity, web users made the leap from text-based surfing to multimedia experiences.

Renamed broadcast.com, the company's breakthrough came in 1999 when 1.5 million viewers logged on for a Victoria's Secret runway show. Yahoo! bought the company for $5.7 billion in stock. Cuban's stake was estimated at $1.5 billion.

He splurged on a mansion simply because he could. He found a beauty: a year-old, 24,000-square-foot colossus spread over seven acres. Behind an 11-foot mahogany door are rooms with 20-foot ceilings, opulent chandeliers and marble floors. There are six bedrooms and six bathrooms—in the main house alone. There's also an 1,800-square-foot, two-bedroom guest house. The grounds also include a swimming pool, tennis court and—of course—a basketball court.

Cuban was in no hurry to decorate. Besides, furniture would've interfered with other household activities: wiffle ball and rollerblading.

Around Thanksgiving 1999, Cuban bought a $40 million private jet that he proudly noted was the most expensive item ever purchased on the internet. Then, on December 19, 1999, he was introduced to the masses with a long feature in the High Profile section of *The Dallas Morning News.*

The final chunk of the article appears under the headline, "Is an NBA team in his future?"

After mentioning an attempt to buy the NHL Pittsburgh Penguins, Cuban said there was one particular franchise "that I'd love to own." The writer brought up "a certain hapless pro basketball team," and Cuban said he was ready to pounce if the owner, Ross Perot Jr., was willing to sell.

Perot was drinking coffee and reading the paper when he stumbled onto those comments. He laughed and admired Cuban's moxie.

FROM THE FRONT ROW TO THE FRONT OFFICE

Mark Cuban's vision of buying the Dallas Mavericks crystallized on November 2, 1999, when he attended the season opener. Although the Mavs beat Golden State by 12, the crowd was lifeless. There were thousands of empty seats.

Perot had bought the club from original owner Don Carter in 1996 mainly to capitalize on a new arena. He endured a bitter, narrow public election in 1998 that would get the place built but still had a few years to wait. So Cuban made Perot an offer he couldn't refuse: $280 million, almost a 125 percent return on his initial $125 million investment. Perot even got to keep a piece of the club, and his company would still be involved in the development around the new arena.

"Money talks," Cuban later said.

The ownership change was drastic.

Perot was a hands-off, suit-wearing, real-estate mogul who, when he bought the team, didn't even know how many players were on the floor at once. In Cuban, the Mavericks got a hands-on, jeans and T-shirt guy who loved the game—remember, it was basketball that sparked the idea that led to his fortune. Running the team would be his top priority.

Cuban had owned season tickets for a long time, eventually landing floor seats. When players were first introduced to the new boss, they couldn't believe it was the loudmouth fan who sat near their bench.

The owner-player relationship flourished quickly. Cedric Ceballos gave Cuban the game ball from the first victory after he took over. Dirk Nowitzki played him one on one and dunked on him. All the players and coaches went to his mansion for a Super Bowl party.

During his wild early days in charge, Cuban floated the idea of Deion Sanders playing for the Mavericks and later talked about hiring Bob Knight. *The Dallas Morning News* tried keeping up with his daily escapades in a box called "Cuban Hoops," while the *Fort Worth Star-Telegram* ran "Cuban's Corner." He gave them plenty of material.

Cuban improved the quality of postgame meals, upgraded hotels and had buffet meals awaiting the team's arrivals. He provided fancy towels and robes, plus crammed their lockers with electronics: a 14-inch flat-screen television hooked up to receive satellite channels, a DVD player, a VCR, video games and headphones. To complement a locker room so luxurious that players might never want to leave, Cuban designed high-back, cushioned leather chairs for the team bench. On an icy night early in his tenure, he sent limousines to chauffeur players to and from Reunion Arena. He later spent $46 million on a new team plane, complete with a weight room, and provided every player with a laptop computer.

"He's quite a dynamo," Carter said a month after Cuban took over. "I might not do everything he would do, but I love seeing someone who is passionate and has a love for the game.

"He sent us flowers on our 40th anniversary and thanked us for being a good partner. I sent a note back to him saying that we're looking forward to it."

Cuban also made drastic changes to the roster. After an ill-fated start with Dennis Rodman, there was a flurry of trades, especially at his first draft. Cuban didn't hesitate to throw in the league-maximum $3 million to seal deals. A sly move was convincing the Detroit Pistons to pull out of a three-way trade that would've sent Christian Laettner to the Los Angeles Lakers, then getting the Pistons to send Laettner to Dallas. Free agents noticed Cuban's first-class treatment of players, and they wanted to be Mavericks, something that hadn't happened for a long time—if ever.

While Cuban was involved, he made it clear that coach/general manager Don Nelson handled all personnel decisions. Nelson was going to retire after the 1999-2000 season, but was so invigorated by the new owner that he signed an 11-year contract that mixed future coaching and front office duties. Of course, the $25 million price tag was pretty convincing, too.

A MAN OF THE PEOPLE

Fans were hooked on Cuban from the start. They loved his Everyman approach, his passion and the way he reached out to them. Cuban absorbed all service charges and handling fees on Mavs tickets, upgraded the seats of people who came to games with their faces painted and bought tickets for fans who traveled to road games. He threw postgame parties and hosted a steak dinner for the 18 fans who went to every home game during the first season he owned the team. Everywhere he went, lines formed for autographs, handshakes and pictures. He was as much of a celebrity as his players. *D* magazine captured the mood by photographing Cuban coming out of a phone booth wearing a Superman T-shirt.

Cuban posted his e-mail address on the scoreboard at games and spent hours every day responding, as he still does. He also started a web site to sell team merchandise (www.mavgear.com) and coined the phrase "Mavs Fan For Life!" or MFFL, which he even turned into his license plate.

Cuban's popularity spread nationally through interviews with newspapers, magazines and TV networks. He appeared on talk shows, attended Michael Jordan's fantasy basketball camp and even sang "Take Me Out to the Ballgame" at Wrigley Field.

NOT JUST ANOTHER OWNER

At first, the rest of the league wasn't quite sure what to make of Cuban.

Other owners immediately appreciated him raising the value of their franchises by overpaying for his. Signing Rodman—and letting the flamboyant forward live at his house—made them wonder, but it didn't stop them from letting him into their fraternity.

Cuban brought fresh ideas to the league office, all aimed at improving the product. He wanted to make NBA games the best entertainment option possible. But his pursuit of perfection often got the best of him. The subjective world of officiating frustrated Cuban to no end, and he let everyone know it. He lashed out against the "star system of refereeing" and hired people to keep track of calls in every game, then offered the information to the league office.

His outspoken comments and other antics resulted in eight fines totaling $1,005,000 and three games missed because of suspensions, all in just his first two years in charge. One writer dubbed his spats with referees "The Cuban Whistle Crisis."

Cuban considered the fines part of the cost of doing business. He called them free publicity and matched each penalty with a charitable donation. They were timely, too, such as $250,000 to prostate cancer research the day coach Don Nelson underwent an operation to fight it, then $375,000 to breast cancer research after Nelson's wife, Joy, was diagnosed with it.

Seven of the fines came during Cuban's first full season as owner, including a $250,000 penalty on the one-year anniversary of his purchase. Fine No. 8 was the biggest—and most memorable: $500,000 for saying the head of officiating couldn't manage a Dairy Queen. The company challenged Cuban to try it, and he gladly accepted.

A few weeks later, he slipped into a zebra shirt to see what it's like on the other side of a whistle by officiating part of a Harlem Globetrotters game.

Referees weren't the only ones bothered by Cuban. After Cuban made comments about the Lakers having a miserly off season, coach Phil Jackson said the Dallas owner "should keep his mouth shut." He used more colorful words to say Cuban didn't know what he was doing. Cuban annoyed Scottie Pippen by rejecting his request for a tour of his mansion and took a war of words with longtime NBA journalist Peter Vecsey onto live television at the 2000 draft. He also was interviewed by *Penthouse*.

It's not often you see a billionaire asking, "Do you want fries with that?"
But Cuban rose to Dairy Queen's challenge, and the owner's
appearance drew long lines—and lots of laughs.
(Ronald Martinez/Getty Images)

Although Cuban has toned it down, his persona keeps growing. He has his own local TV show that's closer to *Saturday Night Live* than *Inside the NBA,* and this past season he was immortalized with his own bobblehead doll.

Love him or hate him, it doesn't matter. The record shows how far the franchise has come since that season opener in November 1999. The Mavericks are winning again, and Mark Cuban is a big reason why.

FINE-BY-FINE TIMELINE

A look at the eight times the NBA reprimanded Mark Cuban during his first two years as owner of the Mavericks. The date listed is when he was punished, not when the incident occurred.

Date: November 14, 2000
Amount: $5,000
Why: Sitting directly behind the bench during a 109-84 loss at Sacramento, Cuban told the refs that fans were laughing at them.
What Cuban said about it: "The policy is to fine anyone who criticizes the officiating. I knew that before I said anything. But it still doesn't address the issue."

Date: November 20, 2000
Amount: $15,000
Running total: $20,000
Why: Cuban didn't like the way a 99-78 loss at Phoenix was being called, especially in the second quarter, when the Mavericks didn't shoot a free throw. Referee Hank Armstrong at one point gestured that Cuban was "this close" to getting in trouble. After the game, Cuban had to be escorted out of the way so the crew could get to their locker room. He kept yelling at referee Hue Hollins anyway.
What Cuban said about it: "The problem I have, and where the league and I are on opposite ends of the planet, are in the tools the league provides the refs to help them improve. ... I guess I will have to grin and bear it and hope they put all the fine money I pay to good use."
Postscript: Nelson told Cuban his outbursts could be doing more harm than good. So Cuban stayed away from the next two games.

Date: November 22, 2000
Amount: $25,000
Running total: $45,000
Why: More of the same, this time stemming from a 116-110 home loss to Seattle. In the final minutes, Cuban thought a shot

by Shawn Bradley that was blocked should've been called goaltending. Then official Gary Benson—who wears No. 30—whistled Bradley for a foul with 42.9 seconds left and Dallas trailing by two. As officials got to their locker room, Cuban was waiting. "Am I mistaken or did No. 30 just hand them the game?" he said. "Nice game, No. 30."

What Cuban said about it: "Although I don't mind paying the fines, this is probably the last. I have had some substantive conversations with the league, and I like some of the steps that are being taken. So we can stop talking about the refs and the processes and talk about basketball."

Postscript: Cuban spent the next two games roaming the stands, even watching from the upper deck.

Date: January 4, 2001, exactly one year since Cuban's purchase was announced
Amount: $250,000
Running total: $295,000—or $806.01 per day
Why: Cuban thought goaltending should've been called on a missed shot by Steve Nash that would've tied a game against Detroit at 106. Michael Finley said officials told him there was no call because the shot had no chance of going in. Dallas lost 107-104. After the teams left the court, Cuban had frozen on the JumboTron a replay that showed a Detroit player's hand touching the rim while Nash's shot was in the air. He gathered photographers to take a picture of it, then said: "The refs were pitiful tonight, and I don't care if I get fined. We're going to find out what the rules are and protest the game." He also accused official Tommy Nunez of trying "to take over the game."

What Cuban said about it: "I think it's great. There is no way we could spend $250,000 to get this type of promotion for the Mavs. The articles will be mostly the same: 'Mark Cuban was fined again, crazy guy, but the Mavs are playing well and are in the playoff hunt.' And tons of people will buy Mavs merchandise and more will come to the games—just like the last time I was fined."

Postscript: The Mavericks did file a protest. No action was taken.
Noteworthy: Cuban's tab surpasses Rodman's career fine total of $193,500. Rodman's biggest was $50,000. Another habitual offender, Charles Barkley, was never hit for more than $20,000.

Date: January 11, 2001
Amount: $100,000
Running total: $395,000
Why: The league office didn't like Cuban sitting on the baseline while watching the Mavericks beat the Timberwolves 106-86 in Minneapolis. Cuban said there were no open seats behind the bench and he did not want to take one of the coaches seats.
What Cuban said about it: "I wasn't aware this was fineable. There isn't a rule against it. They said it wasn't fitting for an owner to sit there. Ridiculous."

Date: February 16, 2001
Amount: $10,000, two-game suspension
Running total: $405,000, suspended from two games
Why: Cuban ran onto the court to help break up a shoving match in the final seconds of a 102-81 victory over Cleveland. The Cavaliers were angry that the Mavericks ran a set play to break 100 points. They did it because fans were chanting "cha-lu-pa," knowing they'd get coupons for free 99-cent chalupas at Taco Bell if Dallas scored 100 and won. Under NBA rules, any team official other than a coach who comes onto the court during a game is automatically suspended for the next two home games and the team is automatically fined $10,000.
What Cuban said about it: "When something like that happens, your instinct isn't to worry what the rule book is going to say."
Postscript: Taco Bell got lots of free publicity. Credit spokeswoman Laurie Gannon for this line: "They shouldn't be fighting over chalupas. They can just go to one of our restaurants and buy one."

Noteworthy: Cuban was fined the equivalent of 10,101 chalupas. The two-game suspension forced him to miss Nelson's memorable return from prostate cancer surgery.

Date: April 13, 2001
Amount: $100,000, one-game suspension
Running total: $505,000, suspended from three games
Why: For a "gesture" during a 111-106 loss at Phoenix that the league told Cuban could be considered intimidating, and for these comments: "If they can't call a fair game with the way the rules are now, how can we expect them to do it if they change the rules? And it's not just today. It's been over and over and over."
Explanation: The rule changes Cuban referred to involved allowing zone defenses starting the following season. The vote was to be taken the next day. Cuban had been planning to support it, but during the same interview in which he uttered the fine-worthy quote, he also said he was changing his mind and would be voting against it. He wound up abstaining.
What Cuban said about it: "I didn't make a derogatory gesture. I jumped up and grabbed my throat after a missed call, and that was it. ... I didn't make a public criticism. I asked the question of how the league was going to introduce new rules if we are having problems with the existing ones."

Date: January 8, 2002
Amount: $500,000, the largest against an individual in league history
Running total: $1,005,000, suspended from three games
Why: More bad-mouthing of the refs after a 105-103 loss to San Antonio. While Cuban's main concerns were that traveling wasn't called several times against Tim Duncan, and that lax officiating was putting his star players at risk, this incident will forever be remembered for what he said about league director of officials, Ed Rush. "Ed Rush might have been a great ref, but I wouldn't hire him to manage a Dairy Queen. His interest is not in the integrity of the game or improving the officiating."

What Cuban said about it: "The fines are the least of what is relevant of what's going on here. Our players are at risk because of all the fouls. ... David Stern is brilliant, diluting any negative response. People get maddest when the truth is spoken, so I guess I'm getting them mad."

Postscript: Cuban takes up a challenge from Dairy Queen to manage one of their stores for a day, and the publicity stunt turns into a huge event.

Noteworthy: Cuban could've bought a Dairy Queen franchise for about $650,000.

20

Hair Color Aside, Mavs Looking Better

DENNIS THE MENACE

The negotiations to sign Dennis Rodman lasted nearly as long as his stay on the team. Rodman flew to Dallas to meet Cuban on January 24, 2000. He signed February 3, but had to party at the NFL's Pro Bowl in Hawaii, so he didn't make his debut until February 10. He was released March 9.

Rodman began his brief residency in Dallas living in Cuban's guest house. Although he paid rent, the NBA nixed it. Cuban also gave "The Worm" permission to skip practices and to arrive for games later than his teammates.

Viewed strictly as a basketball move, signing Rodman made sense. His toughness, defense, rebounding and championship pedigree were all missing ingredients. But Rodman was only interested in self-promotion. He was thrown out of his second game for sitting down on the court, then berated officials as he left slowly. That drew a one-game suspension and a $10,000 fine. He was tossed from his next home game for taunting Utah's Karl Malone and again lingering on the court. That cost him $3,500.

Rodman constantly accused the league office and referees of being out to get him. He even challenged NBA commissioner

*The Dennis Rodman experiment provided great PR,
but did little for the win-loss record.
(NBAE/Getty Images)*

David Stern to a fight, saying, "Let's get into the ring. He gets naked, I get naked and let's go in and get it on, brother."

Fans ate it up.

Rodman's debut drew the second largest crowd in Reunion Arena history and was the most watched Mavericks game on the regional FOX Sports Net in the seven years it had been receiving ratings. People lined up to spend $43 on replica jerseys with Rodman's name and number (70), and they jostled to catch the real thing when he took it off and flung it into the stands while leaving the court.

Still, it didn't take long for him to wear out his welcome. The end came soon after he ripped Cuban for "hanging around the players like he's a coach or something ... he needs to be the owner, step back and put people in who can get this team in the right direction."

Cuban—who had to defend the signing to league officials while they were considering whether to approve him as an owner—said Rodman was released because he wasn't helping Dallas make up ground in the playoff chase. That was true: The Mavericks won seven of the eight games before Rodman suited up, then went 4-9 during his tenure, slipping from eight games out of the last playoff spot to 10. One of the wins came when he was suspended.

"I would do this all again and sign Dennis in a heartbeat," Cuban said when Rodman was released. "It was the right move; we just didn't get the wins we wanted."

For one month, the Mavericks indeed got more publicity than they'd had in years. And people were starting to pay attention to the team and its provocative owner.

As for Rodman, his eccentric career came to an end with his hair dyed blue and green, the Mavs' colors.

FABULOUS FINLEY

Michael Finley already had established himself as Dallas's top player. In February 2000, he was honored as one of the league's brightest, too, by being named an All-Star. His candidacy received a surprising spark: While reserves were being considered, Scottie Pippen said Finley didn't deserve it because he was on a lousy team. Then Finley had 32 points, eight assists and six rebounds in a 113-105 victory over Pippen and the Portland Trail Blazers.

"He brought a lot of attention to the situation, and I just expanded on it," Finley said, which is as close to screaming "In your face!" as he'd ever come.

Finley finished the season with career highs in points, rebounds and assists. He led the team in scoring, steals and assists. He also broke his own franchise record for minutes played, an impressive feat considering he had a painful foot problem that required extensive treatment before and after every game. Teammates appreciated and respected Finley's durability. They all considered him their leader—the quiet, lead-by-example type.

Michael Jordan noticed, too. The two Chicagoans became fast friends through off-season workouts, and when Nike launched its first line of Air Jordan shoes for players other than their namesake, Finley was among six players selected to wear them.

LIGHT AT THE END OF THE TUNNEL

When the 1999-2000 season ended, Leon Smith, Dennis Rodman and the entire disastrous decade of the '90s were in the past—and the future was looking bright.

Dallas went 40-42 and was ninth in the Western Conference. Better yet, the Mavericks were 31-19 after Cuban took over. They won 16 of their last 21 games and nine of their last 10. No wonder coach Don Nelson savored the final win—supposedly the last of his career—by lighting up a victory cigar and proclaiming, "We're the best team in basketball right now."

"It's sad that this team did not make the playoffs, but we've shown that we're capable of playing that well," said Nowitzki, who had started living up to Nelson's hype by more than dou-

Michael Finley, the "deal maker" in the Jason Kidd trade, was the only player to survive Don Nelson's roster purge after he took over as GM. Finley became a two-time All-Star, co-captain and part of the Big Three. (NBAE/Getty Images)

bling his scoring average to 17.5 points per game and finishing second in voting for the Most Improved Player award.

"There will be no excuses next year," Nash said.

But there was one question looming about the upcoming season.

Who would be the coach?

21

Big-Time Big Three

KEEPING NELLIE

Mavs owner Mark Cuban dumped the Don-to-Donnie succession plan. It wasn't that he didn't want Donnie. He still wanted Don.

"There are only about five great coaches in the league, and we won't accept anything less than a great coach," Cuban said. "Nellie is a great coach."

Nelson's resolve to leave began to crack once the team got hot late in the 1999-2000 season. With the team's top players also endorsing his return, the job remained his all along. He accepted May 27, a few weeks after turning 60.

Nelson agreed to be coach and GM through 2002-03, then spend three seasons as GM only and five more as a consultant.

"IT'S PAYBACK TIME"

When the Mavericks opened training camp in October 2000, Cuban already was in postseason form.

"I can just feel the sparks coming off of me," he said. "I can't sleep at night."

The excitement was over a roster that had been seriously re-shaped. By the opener, Dallas had made seven trades involving 25 players and draft picks. The newcomers included veterans Christian Laettner, Loy Vaught, Howard Eisley and rookies Courtney Alexander, Donnell Harvey, Etan Thomas and Eduardo Najera. Najera, the only second-rounder of the group, even earned a spot in the starting lineup.

"I don't just see us scraping to make that last playoff spot," Cuban said. "I really see us competing."

The season marketing slogan was "It's Payback Time." While it mainly meant fighting back against teams that had been kicking the Mavs while they were down, it also indicated a reward to long-suffering fans.

Dallas opened 10-5 and kept rolling. The Mavericks never had a losing record—something not to be underestimated for a team that's last winning season was 1989-90—and never lost more than three in a row.

In the final season at Reunion Arena, Dallas won 53 games, matching the second most in team history, and ended an 11-year playoff drought that was the longest in the NBA.

THE BIG THREE

Michael Finley, Dirk Nowitzki and Steve Nash were the best trio Dallas sports had seen since Troy Aikman, Emmitt Smith and Michael Irvin won a trio of Super Bowls in the mid-1990s. Those Cowboys stars picked up the moniker of "The Triplets." At Reunion Arena, the catchprase was "The Big Three." While lacking creativity, it certainly fit.

Finley was an All-Star again, and Nowitzki was ready to join him. Nowitzki overtook Finley as the team's leading scorer—by only 19 points over 82 games—and led the team in rebounding for the second straight year. It was only the second time the same player ever led the team in points and rebounds for an entire season. Jay Vincent was the first in 1981, during the team's second season. Among Nowitzki's standout games were career bests of 38 points and 17 rebounds against Orlando, 25 points against Detroit in a game he nearly missed because of the flu, then scoring 31 the next night in Boston, going five of seven on three-pointers.

"That young man in the corner has maybe the best stroke I've seen since Larry Bird," raved Boston coach Rick Pitino after witnessing the kind of performance he expected from Nowitzki when he tried drafting him. "He's a terrific basketball player."

Nowitzki wound up on the All-NBA third team, becoming the first Maverick ever named to any of those squads.

Nash's season began in the summer when he captained the Canadian Olympic team to the quarterfinals in Sydney. In Dallas, he finally gave in to Nelson's urging that he shoot more and nearly doubled his scoring average to 15.6 points per game. He also jacked up his assists to 7.3 per game.

Nash was becoming a star off the court, too. His all-energy style made him a fan favorite, and his distinctly ragged hairstyles made him popular with the ladies. He was rumored to be romantically linked to actress-model Elizabeth Hurley and former Spice Girl Gerri Halliwell, both of whom were spotted at Reunion Arena.

BABYFACE

When Donnell Harvey made his Mavericks debut on December 8, 2000, he became the team's first player younger than the franchise.

Dallas officially received the rights to join the NBA on April 28, 1980. Harvey was born August 26, 1980, exactly one month before the Mavericks played their first exhibition game.

NELLIE'S BIGGEST BATTLE

The Mavericks cruised through the first six weeks of the season, building momentum and confidence. Then came a major jolt. Nelson had prostate cancer.

Nelson found out hours before a game in Houston, but didn't tell the team until afterward. He took a week off investigating his options, then underwent surgery in early January. He missed 52 days.

The original plan was for Del Harris, who'd been an NBA head coach for 13 years, to take over. But he deferred to Donnie Nelson. Dallas went 13-8, a .619 winning percentage, under Donnie. They were 20-12 (.625) when Don left.

SHAQ HACKED OFF OR
JUST CLOWNING AROUND?

Nelson timed his return so that he could face Shaquille O'Neal and the Lakers. It was the first time the teams met since a tense game that prompted Shaquille O'Neal to call Nelson a "clown" for the way the Mavericks abusively defended him. (It was Nelson who first devised the Hack-a-Shaq strategy, which involves mercilessly fouling the poor free throw shooter.)

Although a still irate O'Neal said a few days later, "I'm a bigger legend in this game than he'll ever be," he softened his stance once Nelson became ill.

He called to wish Nelson a speedy recovery and repeatedly said, "I love you, Don Nelson," upon arriving in Dallas for Nelson's return game.

Then came their well-orchestrated public reconciliation. Nelson came out for pregame introductions, waited for photographers to surround him, then pulled out a red foam clown nose and squeezed it on. O'Neal walked over, plucked the toy off

Nelson's face and onto his own. A picture of the silly scene still hangs in Nelson's office.

"I am a bit of a clown," Nelson said.

O'Neal had the last laugh as the Lakers won again.

A RED ARMY COUP

On April 4, 2001, the Dallas Mavericks finally signed their top pick from the 1999 draft. Wang Zhizhi hadn't been holding out. He was in China's Red Army.

The 7-foot-1 Wang became the first Asian-born player in league history. He scored six points and grabbed three rebounds in his debut, a victory over the Hawks. He might not have spoken English, but he did understand something very American: The Chalupa Shot. One of his baskets put the Mavericks over 100 points, earning fans free 99-cent treats from Taco Bell.

"He went from 'The new guy from China' to 'The Chalupa Boy,' and that's pretty special around here," Cuban said.

Despite his size, Wang preferred to shoot from the outside. Dallas had plenty of people to do that, so for the rest of the season he was mostly a novelty. His assimilation was slowed the following season because he missed training camp to play for China's national team. The Mavericks allowed that as part of the deal that brought him to the United States.

The wooing of Wang was unique, to say the least. In a first-person article for *Hoop* magazine, Donnie Nelson wrote about a live snake being brought to the dinner table in a cage, then taken to the kitchen and returning as the meal—and cocktails.

"Part of the snake's internal organs—gizzards or whatever—became part of the ceremony," Donnie wrote. "The host placed them in a glass of alcohol, and with his chopsticks mashed it into a green mulch. He then proposed a toast and passed the drink around for everyone to enjoy. What are you going to do? ... I hope he's worth it."

In signing Wang, the Mavericks broke ground that would help Yao Ming join the Houston Rockets as the top pick of the 2002 draft. However, that same summer, Dallas let Wang sign as a free agent with the Los Angeles Clippers after he refused to return to China to help the national team prepare for the world championships.

UNITED NATIONS LINEUP

Wang's arrival let the Mavericks occasionally use a Foreign Five. The other four: Nowitzki (Germany), Steve Nash (Canada), Eduardo Najera (Mexico) and any American.

Cuban joked that the Mavs would be in great shape "if we ever have to play anybody in soccer for a tiebreaker."

Cuban played off on the worldwide flavor by wearing a T-shirt during the 2001 playoffs that featured the phrase "It's Payback Time" in Chinese, German, Spanish and an African dialect. The nationalities increased the following season with the addition of French-born Tariq Abdul-Wahad. In 2002-03, Dallas drafted Mladen Sekularac of Yugoslavia and signed another Frenchman, Antoine Rigaudeau.

American Express turned this theme into a hilarious television commercial in 2003. Nelson is shown speaking to his foreign players in their native tongues—German, Spanish, French and "Canadian." That last one is indicated by Nelson saying, "Ya hoser."

THE (FIRST) BIG TRADE

Despite all the deals Nelson and Cuban had made, the biggest was still to come: an eight-player trade with the Michael Jordan-run Wizards on February 22, 2001.

Washington got rid of Juwan Howard and one of the league's biggest—and worst—contracts, a seven-year, $105 million albatross that had about $40 million over two years remaining.

Cuban didn't care, because Howard was the kind of big man the Mavericks needed. Upgrading the frontcourt was the only chance they had to go anywhere in the playoffs, and Howard was averaging 18.2 points and 7.0 rebounds.

Dallas gave up Courtney Alexander, Hubert Davis, Christian Laettner, Etan Thomas and Loy Vaught. The other players the Mavericks got were Calvin Booth and Obinna Ekezie.

"Michael Jordan ... got a bunch of good guys, and he's cut his payroll," Nelson said. "They gave us an opportunity to acquire a very fine player, and we took advantage of that."

Howard was the fourth option on offense, which would be a serious snub to some players. Howard loved it. He also was happy to be playing alongside Finley, his close friend and off-season workout partner.

"I was one of the guys who helped assemble the Fab Five [in college at Michigan] because I wanted to be surrounded by great players to win a championship," Howard said. "Now to be part of a situation like this, I'm happy."

RETURN TO THE PLAYOFFS:
THE COMEBACK KIDS

Although Dallas won 53 games, it earned only the fifth seed in the Western Conference. That meant starting on the road against the Utah Jazz.

The Mavericks couldn't be too greedy. After all, it had been 11 years since they were in the playoffs and 13 years since they had won a postseason game—not since Game 6 of the 1988 conference finals. The breakthrough was especially sweet for Shawn Bradley and Finley, who were the active leaders in the dubious category "most games played without a playoff appearance."

Dallas got off to a bad start. By losing the first two games of the best-of-five series, the Mavericks were on the brink of elimination and were accused of falling into a "just happy to be here" trap.

Then came Game 3. Dallas led by 11 early in the fourth quarter, only to fall behind 91-90 when John Stockton made a layup with 34 seconds left. Nash, who had seven stitches in his forehead closing a gash opened in a third-quarter collision with Stockton, answered by racing downcourt, spinning away from Stockton and nailing a 10-footer. A steal by Finley led to two free throws and a three-point lead.

Stockton held for the last shot, then threw up a wild three-pointer with five seconds left. Nash got the rebound, and the celebration was on. So was the series. The Mavericks showed off their young legs and athleticism with a 107-77 victory in Game 4. One of their prettiest plays was Finley catching a rebound and while still in the air throwing a baseball-style outlet pass to Nash, who flipped it to a streaking Nowitzki for a dunk over flat-footed Karl Malone.

"We feel we're coming of age," said Nash, who had 27 points. "If we continue improving, we'll reach the stage where we can say, 'We've arrived.'"

Game 5 was back in Salt Lake City. Dallas trailed by 17, then used a 15-2 run to get close in the fourth quarter. The Mavericks were down by one when Finley fed Booth for the go-ahead points with 9.8 seconds left. It was Booth's only basket of the game—and one of the most important in team history, certainly in the last 13 years.

On Utah's final possession, Bryon Russell missed a three-pointer, and Stockton rebounded and passed to Malone for an open jumper from the top of the key. He missed.

Nowitzki sprinted victory laps around the court, while Nelson pumped his fist. There were hugs and high-fives among the small contingent of Mavericks players and fans.

The hometown crowd was stunned to see the Jazz make their earliest playoff exit since 1995. Utah also was the first team to blow an 0-2 lead in a five-game series since Seattle in 1994.

"I never thought I would be a hero," said Booth, who played in just 15 regular-season games. "I just wanted to give us a little boost."

Dallas overcame double-digit deficits in all five games. The Mavs led Game 5 for only 28 seconds.

"We never stopped fighting," Finley said. "As far behind as we got, we knew from the previous games we could come back."

PLAYOFF RUN ENDS IN THE ALAMO CITY

Two days later, the Mavericks were in San Antonio facing Tim Duncan and the Spurs. They never had a chance.

Scoring just 11 points in the first quarter of Game 1, Dallas struggled throughout that game and most of the rest of the series. They were spent—physically and emotionally.

No one expected them to get this far, so they'd already over-achieved. And while they tried pulling off another upset, this wipeout showed how far they still had to go. But there were some bright spots, especially a 112-108 victory in Game 4 that avoided a sweep and made the Mavs 4-0 when facing elimination. It also prevented them from ending their 21 seasons at Reunion Arena with a loss.

San Antonio finished Dallas off by winning Game 5 by 18 points. The Spurs won the others by 16, 14 and 14. In the finale, Finley missed 16 of 17 shots and the Mavs were 0 of 11 on three-pointers. Still, Nowitzki had a career-high 42 points and 18 rebounds in Game 5, capping a superb postseason. He led Dallas in scoring in five of the 10 games and three of the four wins. He had at least 30 points four times, played through food poisoning in Game 3 against San Antonio, then had his right front tooth knocked out in Game 4.

Even though Dallas's season was done, there was plenty of optimism.

"I'm not going to let this diminish our accomplishments," Nash said following the playoff finale. "We'll be better and stronger next year."

22

New-Look Mavs

RELOADING

The 2001 off season was all about fine-tuning the roster. They re-signed Michael Finley for a maximum deal of more than $100 million over seven years and kept Shawn Bradley for a lot less. They signed free agents Adrian Griffin and Danny Manning, then got Evan Eschmeyer after surprisingly losing Calvin Booth to Seattle.

The splashiest move was getting Tim Hardaway in a sign-and-trade deal with Miami. Dallas gave up only a second-round pick. Hardaway was drafted and nurtured to stardom by Don Nelson at Golden State in the early 1990s. Tim was the "T" in the exciting Run-TMC trio that also featured Mitch Richmond and Chris Mullin.

Nelson wanted a full reunion, but Richmond signed with the Lakers and Mullin didn't want to become an assistant coach. Unable to land that trio, the Mavericks moved to keep their own threesome intact. Nowitzki signed a six-year contract extension for more than $90 million, locking up him and Finley through 2007-08.

NEW ARENA, NEW LOGO, NEW UNIFORMS

In 2001-02, the Mavericks got some new clothes and a new logo to show off in their new $420 million home.

For the first 21 seasons, the logo was a slanted blue M with a white cowboy hat hanging over the top right corner, all set on top of a green basketball.

The new look is a circle with a blue basketball on the right and a fierce-looking horse in silver, white and black on the left. Look closely and you'll find a silver M on the black part of the mane. While that image is painted at center court of the new floor and can be found on players' shorts, it's only part of the full logo. The whole package features that image set on top of a silver shield with the word Mavericks in all capital letters, written in blue and black, and a star beneath the circle. A small white strip arches over the horse's head with the word Dallas in small capital letters.

The uniforms are tastefully simple, with a V-neck instead of the traditional tank-top look around the shoulders. "Dallas" is in blue on white home uniforms and white on dark blue road jerseys. That's unique, because most teams go with the city name only on the road and the nickname at home.

As for the arena, American Airlines Center is vastly larger than Reunion. It has more than 1,000 extra seats, 142 luxury boxes and lots of bells and whistles. The amenities—including a practice court—are far superior. A drawback is that most seats are farther from the court.

STRANGE SIGHT: MICHAEL FINLEY IN STREET CLOTHES

The same night that Nelson became the third coach to reach 1,000 wins, another rarity occurred—Finley didn't play. Finley's league-best streak of 490 consecutive games ended because of a sore left hamstring. It was the first time Nelson coached the Mavericks without No. 4 in the lineup.

"I felt naked," Nelson said.

Finley led the league in minutes the previous two seasons and three of the last four. He once played a preseason game hours after having his wisdom teeth pulled. He didn't tell coaches about it until the next day, when they wondered why he'd been lacking energy.

The hamstring problem landed Finley on the injured list for the first time in his career. He missed 13 games—but Dallas went 12-1 without him. That said a lot about a team that once relied solely on Finley.

If anything, Finley's absence proved that the Mavericks were becoming Nowitzki's team. He was the leading scorer in 11 of the games Finley missed, including 10 of the wins. Only two were close, and Nowitzki sealed both. He made four free throws in the final 6.9 seconds of a 106-103 victory over Utah and converted a three-point play with 6.9 seconds left in a 95-94 victory over Denver the night Finley went on the injured list.

"In that situation, Mike usually gets the ball," Nowitzki said. "But he's not here, so they called a post-up play for me."

NELSONS FACE CANCER—AGAIN

During Finley's absence, Nelson was gone for two games, too, because his wife, Joy, underwent an operation to fight breast cancer. A year after his own brush with the disease, Nelson said it was tougher watching his wife endure it.

Both Nelsons were lucky, because their illnesses were detected early. They in turn used their high-profile status to spread the word about routine exams—such as at the All-Star Game, when Nelson coached the Western Conference.

"Early detection saved her life," Nelson said. "She preached early mammograms and took them. Same with me—early detection saved my life."

Joy Nelson had been working on breast cancer prevention since 1992, when she joined the "NBA Wives Saves Lives" project while Don coached Golden State.

ANOTHER TRADE-DEADLINE BLOCKBUSTER

The Mavericks were leading the Midwest Division when the trade deadline arrived. Nelson and Cuban were expected to tweak the end of the bench or do nothing. Instead, they made one of the biggest deals in franchise history.

Juwan Howard, the centerpiece of the previous season's deadline deal, went to Denver with Hardaway, Donnell Harvey and next year's first-round pick in exchange for Raef LaFrentz, Nick Van Exel, Avery Johnson and Tariq Abdul-Wahad. Like the Washington deal, this was a win-win swap. The Mavericks upgraded their roster while dumping a struggling player's salary.

LaFrentz was the showcase player, but he was a risk because he'd be a free agent after the season. The knock on Van Exel was his attitude, which had been a problem before. Johnson and Abdul-Wahad were big cap crushers.

Still, the Mavericks added two potential starters and two potentially solid role players while dropping several others who were no longer good fits.

"I just felt that we needed to get a little deeper," Nelson said. "And we did that."

LaFrentz became an immediate starter. The only problems Van Exel caused were for opposing defenses as he backed up Nash and occasionally joined him in the backcourt. Johnson became the only player on the roster with a championship ring. He was so respected by teammates and coaches that he occasionally led practices. When left off the playoff roster, he became a temporary assistant coach.

MEDIA DARLINGS

With their exciting style, improving record and maverick owner, the Dallas Mavericks became a hot commodity.

A great indication of their new status came when Dirk Nowitzki made the cover of the May 1, 2001, issue of *Sports*

Soaring for a dunk or swishing a three-pointer, Dirk Nowitzki has
become one of the top players in the NBA.
(NBAE/Getty Images)

Illustrated. An action shot was accompanied by the words "Style Points;" beneath it, a smaller headline proclaimed, "Dirk Nowitzki and the high-scoring Mavericks are the best show in basketball." Jinx or not, it was the first time any Maverick got that honor.

Nowitzki was becoming such a star that a mere haircut created, well, a big buzz. After Nowitzki got his long blond locks whacked, Nelson "sold" bags of the strands for donations to breast cancer research. One fan came to a game wearing a mop on his head and holding a sign that read, "I bought Dirk's hair on eBay."

Nash's Q-rating was soaring, too. During the playoffs, he flew to New York to appear on *The Late Show with David Letterman.*

Nash and Nowitzki also both made the All-Star team for the first time, then Nowitzki was named second-team All-NBA and Nash made third team. The insightful Nash also made second team on the All-Interview squad.

HOW SWEEP IT IS

The Mavericks went into the 2002 playoffs with a franchise-best 57 wins, including an NBA-best 26 on the road. Their 105.2 points per game were the most since the 1997-98 Chicago Bulls, and they set a league record for fewest turnovers.

But the Western Conference was still so tough that Dallas was the fourth seed. At least that meant home-court advantage for the first-round series against Minnesota. Dallas took full advantage, winning the first two games at American Airlines Center then stomping the Timberwolves in Game 3 in Minneapolis. With the Big Three combining for 94 points, the Mavericks never trailed in the finale. In fact, Dallas led or was tied for the final 73 minutes, 43 seconds of the series.

This was the sixth playoff series the Mavs had ever won, the first in a sweep. The best part was getting extra time to prepare for the second round.

"When we won the first series last year, it was like we won the championship—and San Antonio took advantage of that," Finley said. "That's not the plan this year. We want to win the next series, and the series after that."

KINGS REIGN

Although Dallas split the first two games of the second-round series against Sacramento, two disturbing trends developed: The Kings were practically scoring at will in the paint, and the Mavericks were relying far too much on their perimeter shooting. Returning home was supposed to help. Instead, Dallas found agonizing ways to lose.

The Mavericks overcame an early 15-point deficit in Game 3 and led in the fourth quarter. The Kings had lost Peja Stojakovich to an ankle injury, and Doug Christie was trying to play through a sprained ankle. But Sacramento still rallied to win.

Then Dallas held a 14-point lead in the second half of Game 4, only to allow a 17-2 run that forced overtime. Even though Chris Webber and Vlade Divac fouled out, the Kings still pulled out the victory.

"We pretty much got what we wanted—we got both of their big guys to foul out—but we couldn't capitalize," Nowitzki said. "I can't believe we lost the game."

Dallas went back to Arco Arena hoping to continue its success while on the brink of elimination that it showed the previous season. But the Kings were just too strong. This time it was Hedo Turkoglu who played the starring role as Sacramento ended Dallas's season the same way San Antonio had the year before—in Game 5 of the second round.

"When you look at history, no team has just turned the corner—not make the playoffs for 10 years and all of a sudden two years later win the championship," Cuban said. "It's disappointing no matter what, but we know we have a great nucleus.

"This is a team that can and needs to stay together for a long, long time. As we play together more and mature and learn how to play together better, there's great things ahead."

SHAKE IT!

The best thing to come out of the playoffs was a new crowd-pleasing act—fat guys who sing and dance.

Known as the Mavs ManiAACs, this collection of 12 heavy-weights and a token thin man won over fans from the moment they came onto the court wearing yellow raincoats, carrying rainbow-colored umbrellas and performing to the tune, "It's Raining Men."

The idea came from the way crowds responded to oversized fans when they were shown on the big screen jiggling during timeouts. Open auditions were held to pick the men who give new meaning to the term "belly dancer." They were taught their steps by Shella Sattler, who also directs the Mavs Dancers.

The ManiAACs ranged in age from 21 to 50 and came from all walks of life. There was a doctor, a firefighter, several teachers, a photographer and a college student.

A year later, the concept was taken a step further with the creation of the GrannyAACs, a dozen ladies ranging in age from 49 to 77 who shook their rears while wearing the team's phone number on the back of their shorts.

The concept was the brainchild of a fan, Linda Pettingell, who e-mailed Cuban with the idea—earning her a spot on the squad.

She wrote: "I am one of the Mavs' biggest female fans and season ticket holders and am standing ready to audition as soon as, and in case one day, you decide that the ManiAACs need some competition—'The Mavs Dancin' Grannies.' Not many would admit to being 61 years old, but I could give those young guns a run for their money ..."

23

A Run to Remember

NEW BANNER, NEW ATTITUDE

A new banner loomed over the Mavericks' practice court in 2002-03. It was a crude reminder of the way the previous season ended.

WESTERN CONFERENCE SEMIFINALS

SACRAMENTO KINGS:
207 FIELD GOALS
WITH
115 LAYUPS AND DUNKS!

In case anyone still wasn't getting the message, coach Don Nelson spent the majority of training camp working on defensive schemes, primarily zones.

"We can write up defenses and we can demand, but they've got to get that job done," Nelson said. "You have to at least look like you're interested in playing defense." Assistant coach Del Harris, whose informal title is "defensive coordinator," made it clear that he didn't expect Dallas to start holding teams in the 80s. The way the Mavericks' offense works, the other team will always get plenty of chances to score. The key, he said, was getting timely stops.

The personnel was mostly the same. The top player move was re-signing Raef LaFrentz for seven years.

The biggest off-season move was promoting Donnie Nelson to president of basketball operations. The change meant Donnie could now take ideas straight to owner Mark Cuban rather than going through the general manager—his dad. It also convinced him to withdraw from consideration for the Denver coaching job.

"The whole thing was about keeping the braintrust together," Cuban said.

14-0!

If anything, a season-opening 119-108 victory over the Memphis Grizzlies left the impression that the defense still needed a lot of work. Then the victories started mounting. At home against Phoenix and Golden State. On the road against Toronto and Chicago. While all were expected, Dallas was 5-0 for the first time and the league's only unbeaten team.

The Mavericks passed their first big test by leading the Detroit Pistons by 52 en route to a 114-75 home victory. Then Dallas plowed through Portland and Cleveland, then Boston and New Jersey on back-to-back nights on the road.

A 98-72 victory over the Lakers—who were without Shaquille O'Neal—made it 11-0. In the game, the three-time defending champions had the lowest shooting percentage in franchise history (30.8 percent on 28 of 91) and came within a basket of their lowest-ever point total.

The franchise record for consecutive wins fell when Dallas beat Houston two nights later. A win at home over Seattle, then a 20-point road win against Detroit (so much for the Pistons getting revenge) upped the streak to 14-0, one shy of the NBA record held by the 1948-49 Washington Capitols and the 1993-94 Rockets.

The Pacers played spoiler with a 110-98 victory on Thanksgiving night.

"We knew we weren't going to go 82-0," Michael Finley said.

The hot start earned the Big Three the joint honor of NBA Player of the Month, and Nelson was named Coach of the Month. The streak also helped Dallas to its best record at the halfway point (33-8) and at the All-Star break (38-10). The Mavs peaked at 38 games over .500, another franchise first.

Then the bubble burst. Finley was hurt in March about the time the schedule got tough. Dallas went through a 6-6 stretch and lost its season-long grip on the NBA's best record. The Mavs finished second in the Midwest Division and landed the third seed in the playoffs. The consolation was that they won a franchise-record 60 games.

The biggest disappointment was failing to end a losing streak against the Lakers in Los Angeles that dated to December 12, 1990. The Mavs blew their first chance in historic fashion, wasting a 30-point lead—27 in the fourth quarter—for a 105-103 loss in December. They were wiped out the next time during the Finley-less period.

SUSPENSION? LET'S PARTY!

Don and Donnie Nelson were suspended from the first two games of the season for attending a workout in Yugoslavia that featured players not eligible for the draft.

So they made the most of their time off.

First came an event billed as "Serve Time with the Nelsons." The duo dressed up in jailbird outfits and watched the opener on television with fans at Dave & Buster's, a restaurant/bar/arcade in Dallas.

Donnie (left) and Don Nelson took their season-opening suspension and turned it into fun for everyone—especially since they picked up the bar tab. (Danny Bollinger/Getty Images)

Then they partied at world-famous honky-tonk Billy Bob's in Fort Worth for the second game. The Nelsons wore blue jeans, black cowboy hats and leather jackets. Donnie Nelson even used a picture from that night on his family's Christmas card.

To prevent the league from punishing the team for this stunt, the events doubled as fundraisers. Team calendars were sold for $10, with proceeds going to local children's organizations.

"WHERE'S FIN?"

Although Finley didn't join Dirk Nowitzki and Steve Nash in Atlanta for the 2003 All-Star Game, he wasn't forgotten. Cuban rented a billboard alongside the interstate highway from Hartsfield International Airport toward downtown Atlanta and posted the message: "Where's Fin?" Cuban also bought a full-page ad in the *Atlanta Journal-Constitution* that was a subtle advertisement for fans to watch the All-Star Game on TV. That message, however, was overwhelmed by the headline: "It's Dirty and Nasty and could've been downright Filthy." Below large pictures of Dirty (Dirk), Nasty (Nash) and Filthy (Finley) was the line: "It's OK, it's the All-Star Game. Go ahead and love them like we do."

Nowitzki and Nash made their Finley tributes on the court. Both wrote "Fin 4" on their shoes.

"We think he should be here as much as me and Nash," Nowitzki said. "We wanted to show him some love."

Cuban also showed Nash and Nowitzki some love by putting up another billboard that read, "Dirty and Nasty Time in Hotlanta." It was located downtown, near the site of the game.

After the season, Nowitzki was named second-team All-NBA, with Nash making the third team.

PERFECTION

Since Rolando Blackman made 45 straight free throws in November 1991, no Maverick had even made 37 in a row.

Until 2002-03.

Nash set a new mark by hitting 49 in a row from December 2 to December 20. Then, from January 2 through January 23, Nash hit 47 straight. Those streaks helped the Mavs challenge the NBA record for free throw accuracy by a team. They finished at 82.9, just missing the mark of 83.2 set by the 1989-90 Boston Celtics.

Dallas celebrated another kind of perfection at the box office. For the first time in franchise history, the team sold every ticket to every game. That turnout was part of the reason that in August 2003, *The Sporting News* named Dallas the best NBA city.

DIRK AND STEVE: INTERNATIONAL IMPACT

There's little doubt that Nash is the best basketball player to come from Canada and that Nowitzki is becoming Germany's best hoop export. Some recent events support their lofty status.

Nowitzki was named the MVP of the 2002 world championships for leading Germany to the bronze medal, its first of any color at this event. Nowitzki finished second in voting for a similar honor among all German athletes. While beaten by record-setting ski jumper Sven Hannawald, he beat out Formula One driver Michael Schumacher and Oliver Kahn, captain of the national soccer team. Nowitzki was voted 2002 Player of the Year by Italian sports magazine *La Gazetta dello Sport*. And spurred by Nowitzki's popularity at home, seven German broadcasters began providing two live NBA games every week in 2003.

Nash was named Canada's male Athlete of the Year for 2002, an honor never given before to a basketball player.

Another unique honor the pals shared was having Lego mini-figurines cast in their image. They were among 24 NBA players depicted in the collectibles released in January 2003.

In April, they did something distinctly American: throwing out the first pitch at a baseball game. Dirk took the mound at The Ballpark in Arlington wearing a No. 41 Texas Rangers jersey and threw to Steve, who was behind the plate wearing No. 13. The pitch was a little high, but Nash snagged it. They left the field celebrating as if they'd just hit a game-winning three-pointer.

ARE YOU READY TO RUMMMMMBLE?

Cuban couldn't take it any more. After being on his best be-havior all season—no fines!—the owner appeared to have snapped during a timeout in the second quarter of a physical game on April 1. He stalked onto the court and confronted a referee dur-ing a timeout. Already wearing a football-style Mavs jersey, Cu-ban tried tackling the ref, then got him into a headlock. A trainer and backup center Evan Eschmeyer rushed over to break it up.

Most people in American Airlines Center were amazed, es-pecially assistant coach Del Harris. Then the public address an-nouncer reminded everyone what day it was: April Fool's.

The real officials were among the few in on the prank. They stood by watching and laughing.

SURVIVING A BIG SCARE

A wonderful regular season set off a great start in the play-offs. The underachieving, squabbling Portland Trail Blazers seemed ripe to be swept. They lost Derek Anderson to a knee injury early on in the series, and Scottie Pippen was out with one, too. Sure enough, the Mavericks beat Portland in three straight games to open the best-of-seven series. One more win and it was on to the second round.

Then came the biggest scare in Mavericks history. Dallas lost and lost, then lost again. They went from 3-0 to 3-3, setting up a winner-take-all finale—and some sleepless nights.

"I went home and pulled down the blinds," Nick Van Exel said. "I didn't want to be seen. It's an embarrassing feeling to be up 3-0 and then lose three in a row."

Facing the chance of becoming the first NBA team to ever blow such a cushion, point guard-turned-assistant coach Avery Johnson gave a pep talk about desire prior to Game 7. The word he used most was "will," underlining it four times on a message board.

His teammates responded by driving the lane, banging for rebounds and playing defense better than they had all series. Nowitzki bounced back from a four-point stinker in Game 6 to score 31, including a three-pointer with 1:21 left that ended any doubts.

"We worked hard all season to get the home-court advantage," Nowitzki said, "and we used that advantage today."

AN EXEL-ENT SERIES

Van Exel was tired of all the talk about how much better the Sacramento Kings were than the Mavericks. He'd heard it all season from Nelson, and after a lopsided loss in Game 1, he was hearing it from everyone else.

So going into Game 2, Van Exel told his teammates to adopt a new philosophy: "F 'em."

Van Exel wanted the Mavs to forget about the Kings and focus only on themselves. If Dallas played to its potential, Sacramento couldn't keep up, he insisted.

He was right. In Game 2, Dallas led 44-40 after one quarter and scored a playoff-record 83 points by halftime en route to a 132-110 win. Van Exel scored 36 points in 30 minutes, making eight of his first nine shots, including three straight three-pointers during a 30-7 run in the second quarter.

While Dallas's confidence soared, the Kings were further wounded by Chris Webber hurting his left knee in the third quarter. He didn't return for the rest of the series.

Van Exel was even better in Game 3, scoring 40 points—the most ever by a Mavs reserve—in a double-overtime victory. But the Kings answered the next day in Game 4, and the teams split the next two games, too, with Dallas losing Game 6 despite Van Exel scoring 35.

Once again, the Mavericks used their home-court advantage. Dallas led by five at halftime and remained ahead the entire sec-

Nick Van Exel came to Dallas with the reputation of a troublemaker. He left in August 2003 as a fan favorite after being the high-scoring emotional savior of a second-round playoff series against Sacramento. (NBAE/Getty Images)

ond half, cruising into the conference finals for the second time in franchise history and the first time since 1988. Finley celebrated by giving Nowitzki a piggyback ride to the locker room.

Van Exel averaged 25.3 points per game in the series with 4.4 assists and 3.9 rebounds—all while coming off the bench. Nelson unabashedly called him the team's best player in the series and there was talk of expanding the Big Three nickname to a Big Four.

WHAT MIGHT'VE BEEN

Four wins from the finals quickly turned into three as Dallas rode an incredible streak of 49 straight free throws to overcome an 18-point deficit and beat the San Antonio Spurs in Game 1 of the Western Conference finals. The Spurs got even by winning Game 2 and were on their way to winning the next one when something worse happened to the Mavericks. They lost Nowitzki to a sprained left knee.

As badly as he wanted to play each of the next three games, Nelson wouldn't allow him to risk his promising future. Nowitzki realized he wouldn't have been much help anyway as just standing during Game 5 caused the knee to tremble.

Still, the pain was worth it for the excitement of that fifth game. Dirk-less Dallas was facing elimination, having lost Game 4 then falling behind by 19 in the first half of Game 5. They were still down 17 with 9:27 left in the third quarter.

What followed is one of the greatest comebacks in team and maybe even NBA playoff history. Down that much without their leading scorer and rebounder when a loss would've ended their season, the Mavericks rallied to win—by 12.

The excitement continued in Game 6 as the Mavs led by 13 with 10:53 to go. Another Game 7 seemed almost certain.

Then "the bottom just dropped out," Nelson said.

Dallas went over eight minutes without scoring, missing seven straight shots and turning the ball over six times. The Spurs took advantage with a 23-0 run that featured three three-pointers by Steve Kerr.

At a dead ball with 1:01 left, Finley headed to the bench biting the collar of his jersey. Nelson met him at the sideline and they hugged. When the game ended, a franchise-record crowd of 20,812 stood and clapped. Nash was the last player to leave the court, and he slowly made a 360-degree turn, applauding back. It was reminiscent of the mutual admiration between the fans and players that started with the finale of the inaugural season.

"We have a lot to be proud of," Nash said. "At the same time, we didn't reach our goal, so it hurts. We were so close to going to the finals."

There was no shame in losing to the Spurs, especially without Nowitzki. Although Dallas won the same number of games as San Antonio, the Spurs won the Midwest Division and were the top seed in the West because of the tiebreaker. They had the NBA Coach of the Year and the MVP, and they went on to beat the New Jersey Nets in six games to claim the championship.

KEEPING NELLIE, PART TWO

Nelson coached the 2002-03 season knowing he was under contract with the Mavericks for eight more years—but none as head coach. So when things were going good, he mentioned that he'd like an extension. Cuban said to wait until after the season.

Had the playoffs turned out differently—like having completed the collapse against Portland—maybe Nellie wouldn't have been invited back. But coming off an oh-so-close run at the championship, Nelson signed on for three more years, matching the length of his GM deal.

In typical Mavs fashion, though, it wasn't lacking drama. Cuban made his welcome-back offer right after the Spurs series, but Nelson spent some time at his home in Maui before deciding whether he wanted to accept the offer. The answer finally came in late June—Yes.

SO LONG, NICK; HELLO ANTAWN AND TRAVIS

The summer of 2003 wasn't going so well for the Mavericks. Their top free agent target, Alonzo Mourning, indicated that he was Dallas-bound but went to New Jersey instead, joining fellow free-agent Jason Kidd. So much for Kidd's interest in returning to the Mavs.

Other big men—including Jermaine O'Neal, Karl Malone, and Brad Miller—wound up elsewhere, too. Making Dallas's inactivity seem worse was the fact that the Spurs, Lakers, and Kings all added players who seemed to improve their rosters.

Then, in mid-August, the Mavericks made their big move— a nine-player trade with Golden State that added inside scoring and rebounding in the form of Antawn Jamison, Danny Fortson, and Chris Mills. Dallas also received Jiri Welsch.

The downside to the trade was that Dallas gave up Van Exel and Avery Johnson, along with Evan Eschmeyer, Popeye Jones, and Antoine Rigaudeau. Besides losing Van Exel's scoring and tenacity and Johnson's locker-room presence, it also meant there was no one left to back up Nash.

Luckily, point guard Travis Best was still on the market. Within days he signed a one-year deal for the veteran minimum. An assist goes to Best's mother, Bobbie, who had never before suggested to her son what to do with his career. This time, though, she made an exception. She told Best to forget about trying to get more money elsewhere and to sign with Dallas because he was such a good fit.

"I'm really confident," Cuban said after the moves were completed, "[that] we've improved a 60-win team."

Management's work was done. The Big Three remained intact, and they had their best supporting cast yet. The 2003-04 season couldn't start soon enough.